A Guide to Historic Missions and Churchs of the Arizona-Sonora Borderlands

RICHARD J. MORGAN JR.

Photography by Frank Grabas & T. Brian Walter

Adventures in Education, Inc.
Tucson

Maps are by Richard J. Morgan, Jr.

Photographs are by Frank Grabas, T. Brian Walter, Chris
Jaime, Michelle Richards, and the author. Except for the
author's work, credit for specific photographs is included with
captions.

Sketches of Colonial-era people are by Debra Oldham
Cover and Book Design by Scott Norris
Printed in the United States by Arizona Lithographers
ISBN 0-9648706-0-6
Library of Congress
Catalog Card Number: 95-80598

Outside front cover, counterclockwise from top right:
Franciscan symbol,
San Ignacio churchtower bell,
Opodepe church,
photos by Grabas.

Outside Back cover: photo of author at Guévavi by Walter

Contents

A detailed view of the ornate plaster relief on the ceiling above the choir loft of the church of San Pedro y San Pablo de Tubutama in the Altar Valley, Sonora (Walter).

Preface

The idea for this book sprang from the delight I felt in first encountering the historic churches of the Arizona-Sonora Borderlands. Although I had read in advance about many of these places, I was unprepared for the diversity in the physical character of what I found upon my visits. The richness of this cultural legacy, scattered about the sparsely populated villages and towns of the borderlands region, sparked a desire in me to share what I had seen and learned about with others.

My intention has been to portray these old churches in their historical context. To do this I have relied heavily on the efforts of the most important scholars in this subject field. This book, then, is a unifying work that summarizes earlier research and presents the most visually interesting of this material in an attractive format with the intent of stimulating popular interest in the subject matter. Its unique scholarly contribution to the field of books generally available on the Arizona-Sonora Frontier missions is the attention devoted to missions established in Sonora before Padre Kino's arrival, most notably those of the Sonora, San Miguel, Moctezuma and Bavispe River Valleys. In this regard I have drawn most heavily on two out-of-print works in the field, Paul Roca's *Paths of the Padres Through Sonora* and George Eckhart's and James Griffith's *Temples of the Wilderness.*

The central focus of the visual imagery presented in this work is the serene beauty of what physically remains for the eye to enjoy today. Photographs are predominantly the work of Frank Grabas and T. Brian Walter, enthusiastic professionals who were novices to the subject but dedicated to capturing what they were seeing for the first time. Photographs of the missions are supported by historical text, map illustrations, and sketches of personalities of the period.

This book was made possible in part by a grant from the Arizona Humanities Council. I am also indebted to several scholars who contributed to this work by offering constructive criticism and content ideas. Most notable in this regard are Mardith Scheutz-Miller, Oscar Martínez and James Officer. My understanding of the Arizona missions was enriched through conversation with David Yubeta and Don Garate of the Tumacácori National Historical Park. My appreciation for rural Sonora was enhanced by Juan and Teresa Nuñez who shared their knowledge of the unique cultural history of Bacadéhuachi, Sonora.

I am also grateful to my family and friends who supported me in this project. My wife Sharon offered constant sympathy while nobly tolerating my eccentricities. My son Ben and my good friend Jim McIntosh proofread the manuscript and offered suggestions. Other friends helped in a variety of ways. Lorraine "Nay Nay" Pipkin reviewed sections of the work and provided me with helpful feedback on reader appeal. Cassie Feng gave charitably of her free time to convert my writing into a useful software programming format.

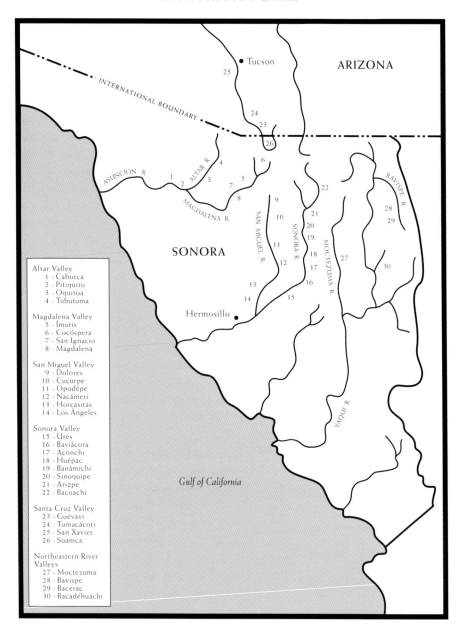

ARIZONA

Tucson

25

INTERNATIONAL BOUNDARY

24

23

26

ASUNCIÓN R.

ALTAR R.

MAGDALENA R.

4

6

1

2

3

5

7

8

9

22

BAVISPE R.

28

29

SONORA

SAN MIGUEL R.

SONORA R.

MOCTEZUMA R.

10

21

20

19

18

17

16

27

30

11

12

13

14

15

Hermosillo

YAQUI R.

Gulf of California

Altar Valley
  1 - Caborca
  2 - Pitiquito
  3 - Oquitoa
  4 - Tubutuma

Magdalena Valley
  5 - Ímuris
  6 - Cocóspera
  7 - San Ignacio
  8 - Magdalena

San Miguel Valley
  9 - Dolores
  10 - Cucurpe
  11 - Opodépe
  12 - Nacámeri
  13 - Horcasitas
  14 - Los Ángeles

Sonora Valley
  15 - Ures
  16 - Baviácora
  17 - Aconchi
  18 - Huépac
  19 - Banámichi
  20 - Sinoquipe
  21 - Arizpe
  22 - Bacoachi

Santa Cruz Valley
  23 - Guévavi
  24 - Tumacácori
  25 - San Xavier
  26 - Suamca

Northeastern River
Valleys
  27 - Moctezuma
  28 - Bavispe
  29 - Bacerac
  30 - Bacadéhuachi

Introduction

General histories of the United States rarely give much attention to the early Spanish settlement of the region that, today, encompasses the borderlands shared by the United States and Mexico. Most illustrated books available on the Spanish colonial missions have focused on historic churches on the northern side of today's international border, leaving the churches on the Mexican side in relative obscurity. There are some books which treat the colonial-era missions established by the Jesuit Padre Kino. This work, however, goes well-beyond these, incorporating the missions established by Kino's predecessors and colleagues in the San Miguel, Sonora, Moctezuma and Bavispe Valleys. The churches which remain in these valleys are all within a day's drive of the Arizona-Sonora Border.

This book is a reference resource and a travel guide. The photos will be especially appealing to the "armchair traveler," while the maps and travel tips will be helpful to those who are motivated to move beyond the armchair and experience, firsthand, the fascinating visual legacy of the early missionaries.

The Jesuits and Franciscans who participated in the Spanish colonization of the Americas undertook a grand experiment. They sought not only to convert native Americans to Catholicism but to establish an institutional framework for a close relationship between religion and daily life. The missionaries pursued these goals in the Arizona-Sonora Borderlands through the establishment of a network of centers of teaching and worship that ranged in nature from humble temporary chapels to enduring mission complexes.

Until the Gadsden Purchase of 1853, all territory of the Arizona-Sonora Borderlands had been part of the political entity of Sonora. Sonora was established in 1640, as a province of New Spain. In 1776, its capital, Arizpe, became the seat of government for the entire northern Spanish colonial frontier. After 1821, with the achievement of Mexican independence from Spain, Sonora became a state of Mexico.

The arrival of the missionaries into the Arizona-Sonora Borderlands followed closely on the heels of the first European explorers. The Spanish adventurer Álvar Nuñez Cabeza de Vaca is generally credited as the first European to pass through what is today the U.S. Southwest. He and a companion, a Moorish slave named Esteban (or Estevanico), were part of an expedition that, in 1527, had been shipwrecked in the Gulf of Mexico along the Texas coast. They and some other survivors began walking overland in search of a way back to Spanish territory.

Vaca, Estevanico, and two other crew members finally made contact with other Spaniards in the Mexican interior in 1536 after an incredible eight-year odyssey of wandering. Their exact route is unknown. However, it is commonly

Depiction of Álvar Nuñez Cabeza de Vaca and his companion Esteban ("Estevanico") during their wanderings in the wilderness (Oldham).

believed that they traveled westward from the Texas coast as far as eastern Arizona before turning southward into Mexico. Upon encountering their countrymen, they told colorful stories that quickly motivated more purposeful explorations northward from the Mexican interior.

The Franciscan missionary Fray Marcos de Niza was the first to undertake such a venture in the year 1539. Niza was primarily interested in finding souls to convert to Christianity. He backtracked along the route that Vaca had followed into Mexico, relying on Vaca's former companion Estevanico as a guide. Niza's journey was cut short by the death of Estevanico and danger from hostile Native

Likeness of the Franciscan missionary Fray Marcos de Niza, first
European to purposefully explore into modern-day Arizona (Oldham).

Americans. However, it is generally believed that he reached as far north as west
central New Mexico. In the process, he located the potential converts he sought.
More important to the general course of history, his tales stimulated further
Spanish interest in the northern region.

The following year, Niza accompanied Don Francisco Vásquez de Coronado
along the same general route and beyond. Coronado's main goal was finding
plunderable treasure. He returned two years later, unsuccessful in his quest. The
sites of mythical wealth he had been searching for had proven to be of little
exploitable value. Still, he traveled as far north as modern-day Wichita, Kansas

and paved the way for further Spanish exploration into the region. In the same time-frame, his countryman Hernando De Soto was meandering from Florida along a convoluted course that generally led him westward, into modern-day Arkansas. It is notable that the Coronado and De Soto expeditions into the North American interior were completed a full 65 years before the founding of the first English colony of Jamestown, Virginia.

Spanish colonization in the Americas progressed slower than exploration. But by the time the English founded Jamestown, the Spanish had already established settlements in northern New Mexico. And in 1775, the year before the American Revolution, Spanish colonists were enroute overland from Tubac, Arizona, to found the first community in the San Francisco Bay area.

The Spaniards, moving northward into what is today the U.S.-Mexico border region, pursued expansion differently than did the North American pioneers who were heading westward from the Atlantic Seaboard. Perhaps most notable in this regard was the use of religion by the Spaniards to pacify Native Americans. Whereas the English marginalized the natives they encountered and generally excluded them from their transplanted European society, the Spanish actively assimilated the indigenous peoples into a colonial society that preserved the values and Catholic beliefs they had brought from Spain. They did this, largely, through the Catholic mission system.

As Spanish explorers roamed the unmapped lands of North America looking for treasures and routes to the Far East, they were generally accompanied by missionaries interested in locating concentrations of native peoples for religious conversion. Often these missionaries played important roles in expeditions as cartographers. Sometimes they were explorers in their own right.

Once a new territory was chosen for settlement, missionaries and small troops of soldiers entered first, establishing military outposts (presidios) and missions. The central role of the soldiers was to provide a physical force to maintain discipline. The central role of the missionary was to instill a faith and attitude among the native peoples that would minimize the actual need to use force in pacifying and preparing a region and her peoples for the arrival of settlers. Missions were sometimes founded without military escort or with only a token escort. In some places, they were established well before presidios were built. Ultimately, however, the availability of troops somewhere nearby became important to the survival of most missions if for no other purpose than to protect them from marauding nomadic peoples, most notably Apaches.

The mission system was established through the efforts of international Catholic orders within limitations imposed by the Spanish Crown. Characteristically, missions were communities organized around agrarian economic activity and a religious-oriented social system. The guiding philosophy of the social system was Christianity as articulated by the resident missionary. Two Catholic orders were most important to the mission system featured in this work, the Franciscans and the Jesuits.

Early Exploratory Routes

It is supposed that Fray Marcos de Niza's route in 1539 followed the Sonora River Valley in Mexico and the San Pedro Valley in Arizona north to the Zuni Pueblo city in New Mexico identified with the legendary city of Cíbola. Coronado probably followed this same route in 1540. Coronado, however, continued beyond New Mexico into what is today Texas, Oklahoma, and Kansas.

With the passage of time the mission system became obsolete. Its demise was gradual, caused by factors discussed in subsequent chapters. Nevertheless, this system left a delightful visual legacy as well as an important social one. In some cases, the mission churches continue to serve the local populaces today.

This work seeks to illustrate the simple architectural beauty of what remains of the mission system in the Arizona-Sonora Borderlands. It also presents the historic context in which these missions were established, thrived, and, finally, declined in importance to the overall way of life in the region.

Each of the early missionary orders used distinctive symbolism for self-identity. This Franciscan symbol, in the form of a relief carving, is found over the main entrance of the mission church of San Pedro de Aconchi in the Sonora Valley. The design consists of a cross with two affixed hands. The sleeveless arm belongs to Christ and the sleeved one to St. Francis of Assisi. A Franciscan cord overarches the cross. The heart and floral fringe are not a standard part of the symbol (Grabas).

Chapter 1
The Spanish Crown
and The Catholic Church

Columbus' initial voyage across the Atlantic was commissioned by the Spanish Crown with the specific objective of finding a new route to the Orient, one that would be more profitable and less complicated than the eastward route cluttered with and obstructed by the competition presented by other countries and other commercial interests. More generally, the Crown was seeking to extend its political and economic power and influence throughout the known world and to absorb undiscovered, unclaimed territories. Columbus' discoveries would open the way for the colonization of an immense new territory, the Americas, an undertaking that Spain would pursue with great energy over the course of the ensuing three centuries.

Spain's political and socioeconomic system during this period was conservative, centralized, authoritarian, and paternalistic. She was ruled by a king who shared power with a landed elite and the Catholic Church. It was an uneasy partnership. The landed nobility vied with the Monarchy for political and economic power. The Catholic clergy was the single richest element within society and held the power to define moral righteousness. The conservative Catholic Church discouraged the changes necessary for progress and encouraged Spain's participation in warfare in support of the spread of papal influence.

After King Ferdinand's death in 1516, a series of Hapsburg kings ruled Spain for 184 years. They engulfed Spain in almost uninterrupted warfare, mismanaged her economic potential, and otherwise squandered her resources. By the end of the 16th Century, Spain was in decline as an international power. She would subsequently regain some vitality under the Bourbon dynasty, but the effect would be fleeting.

Spain's strategy for the Americas, at least initially, was essentially short-term and exploitive. She felt pressed to extract everything of immediately useful value from these new lands to meet war debts and other expenses. She initially sent mostly men, soldiers and missionaries. Later, she would send women and families and encourage developmental economic activity. But the Spanish Crown would remain relentless in the draining of her colonies of as much value as possible throughout the colonial period.

The Spanish Monarchy shared with the Catholic Church the desire to incorporate the indigenous peoples of the Americas into an enduring colonial society. However, the motives of the two hierarchies were somewhat different. The Church viewed the native Americans as children of God in need of religious conversion. The Crown primarily viewed them as exploitable labor and tax resources. As Catholics, Spain's rulers were morally bound to cooperate, at least in principle, with the Church in a paternalistic, constructive approach to the social assimilation of native peoples. Still, civil authorities in New Spain rarely acted with this sense of moral obligation. It was largely left to the missionaries to be the protectors of the Indians while serving as agents of both the King and God.

The first missionaries in New Spain, a contingent of 12 Franciscans, arrived in 1524. They were followed by Dominicans and Augustinians in the 1530's. The first Jesuits arrived in 1572. The Franciscans were old hands at missionary work. The Jesuits were a dynamic new order that had only recently been formed.

The Jesuits were generally considered to be the most authoritarian and internally disciplined of all the Catholic missionary orders. They were directed by a single executive authority in Rome, the Jesuit General. The Order organized the targeted "missionary world" into provinces, of which New Spain was one. Each province was headed by a "Provincial". The provinces were further divided into rectorates which were headed by rectors (sometimes called "Superiors"). Each rector was responsible for a chain of missions. A mission was composed of a *cabecera* (or headquarters), where a resident missionary was stationed, and a cluster of *visitas* (or mission stations) which were maintained by Christian lay people who attended to the religious needs of the local faithful in the missionary's absence and who assisted him during his periodic visits to preach and dispense sacraments.

The Provincial employed experienced Jesuits, as an extension of his personal control, to visit the rectorates on a periodic basis. These "visitors" were delegated limited powers to influence local activities in the missionary field. Their work generally consisted of communicating instructions from the Provincial to rectors, offering advice to the rectors and their subordinates, and reporting observations as well as requests from the field to the Provincial upon returning from trips. In 1725, the functions of such visitors were incorporated into the office of a "Visitor General" who became, in effect, a roving vice-provincial.

Catholic orders like the Jesuits and Franciscans were international organizations which cooperated with the Crown because of the traditional symbiotic relationship between the Monarchy and the Church. The Jesuit Provincial was obligated to be responsive to the civil government established in New Spain, but he did not belong to the King. His first loyalty was to the Jesuit General in Rome.

The Spanish Crown was determined to limit papal influence and to generally preclude the involvement of foreigners in matters of the state. Consequently, it placed restrictions on the operations of the Catholic orders in its territories. For example, until the 1660's, the Crown only authorized Spanish members of these Catholic orders to operate in New Spain. Nevertheless, the Jesuit order sometimes assigned non-Spaniards, thinly disguised as Spaniards, to missionary posts there.

Even when civil and missionary authorities cooperated, there was a natural tension between the two created by different perspectives and goals. The Crown ultimately expelled the Jesuits from all Spanish domains. The reasons were numerous. The ideological fervor of the Jesuits, their non-compromising approach in maintaining paternalistic authority over Native American converts, their closely knit, highly disciplined organization, and their strong allegiance to the Pope all combined to create powerful enemies in New Spain and in the royal court of Spain. Finally, in 1767, Charles III ordered their deportation. The Franciscans, who were considered by the Crown to be more manageable, inherited the Jesuit missionary charter in New Spain.

The Franciscans responded to the challenge admirably. They rebuilt or otherwise renovated the frontier missions of which they took charge. Further, they went on to establish 21 other missions in what is today the state of California. However, some of the Jesuit missions were not incorporated into the Franciscan system. And, the maintenance of the mission system ultimately proved to be an overwhelming task for the Franciscans as increasing limitations were imposed on their authority and activities by, first, Spain and, later, by the newly independent Mexican government.

Missions were religious-based communities organized around agrarian activity. Architectural style and layout of buildings and rooms varied greatly from site to site. While the church (or chapel) was always central to the community, it was just one of the numerous functional structures incorporated into the community complex. Other structures commonly included the priest's quarters with attached kitchen, store rooms, a blacksmith's shop, loom rooms, milling rooms, and living quarters for neophytes. This miniature representation of a mission is located in the museum at Tumacácori National Historical Park, near Tubac, Arizona (Walter).

Depiction of early contact between a European missionary and a Native American tribal leader along the Spanish colonial frontier (Oldham).

Chapter 2
The Land and its Native Peoples

Physical and Biotic Characteristics

The diverse physical character of the Arizona-Sonora Borderlands varies from arid stretches of shifting sand dunes to sub-humid rugged mountains. On the Mexican side of today's border, the region is geographically divided along a north-south line into two areas; a western desert (*El Desierto*) and an eastern mountainous highlands (*La Serrana*). The course of the San Miguel River marks the boundary between these two areas. On the Arizona side of the border, the terrain and climate are largely a continuation of the desert to the south.

The desert topography consists of plains and hills interdicted by rivers which, in Mexico, originate in the eastern highlands. The fertile soil and rich vegetation of the river valleys contrast sharply with the relatively muted character of the desert. Parts of the rivers are intermittent during dry seasons when waters disappear in desert gravels. Summers are very hot, with little relief at night. Winter temperatures are generally mild, with occasional cold waves and night frosts.

Despite the desert's aridity, its terrain supports a broad variety of vegetation, much of it useful to the sustainment of wildlife and human habitation. Plantlife includes a wide range of cactus, shrubs and low trees. In river floodplains, taller trees, like the cottonwood and willow, can be found. Deer, javelina, coyote, rabbit, and a variety of rodents populate the desert.

The highlands are characterized by a series of mountain ranges separated by elongated fertile valleys carved by several rivers and their tributaries. The mountains become increasingly rugged eastward where they form the west flank of the Sierra Madre Occidental. Summers are hot, but milder than in the desert. Winter temperatures are relatively cool, with lower temperatures at higher elevations. Night frosts are common in the winter.

The highlands sustain a broader range of vegetation and wildlife than does the desert. In many areas, cactus and scrub trees share space with tall trees and thick grasses. At higher elevations, evergreens and oak are common. Animals common to the desert are also indigenous to the highlands. Additionally, the Serrana is home to bear, wolf, and a variety of mountain cats.

Both desert and highlands experience the same general rainfall pattern, but the highlands get more rain. Moreover, desert rainfall is more sporadic and localized. The heaviest rainfall is in the summer between July and September. A substantial but lighter rainfall occurs in the winter, between late November and early February. These rainy periods are spaced by prolonged dry spells.

The Native Peoples

Only isolated pockets of Native American culture exist today in the Arizona-Sonora Borderlands. Racial intermixing occurred quickly in the Spanish Colonial Period.

Most of the Native American groups that the Spaniards encountered here shared similar cultural traits and belief systems. Their social organizations were simple and decentralized. Their languages differed somewhat but most groups spoke one of two Uto-Aztecan languages: Piman or Ópatan. Their subsistence activities varied somewhat but they all farmed and were, to some degree, hunters and gatherers. They were largely sedentary. Differences were mostly attributable to environmental circumstances.

There were some notable exceptions to this characterization. Some groups in the Sierra Madres spoke Tarahumaran, another Uto-Aztecan language. Bands of nomadic Indians along the north Mexican coast (the Seri) and other groups along the northern and western rims of Spanish expansion into Arizona (for instance, the Yuma) spoke variants of the Hokan language. After the mid-seventeenth century, the borderlands were increasingly penetrated by bands of migrating Apaches that followed a nomadic life style and spoke a variant of the Athapaskan language.

The Spanish found it useful to give different names to the natives they encountered, largely based on the language and dialect differences between them. Piman and Ópatan speakers were differentiated into seven discrete groups. Such distinctions were applied to Hokan and Athapaskan speakers as well. Other factors contributed to these distinctions, to include physical distances between the settlements of these groups and feelings of self-identity that this physical separation fostered. There were also variations in size and concentration of native settlements and differences in the relative sophistication of farming techniques that various groups employed.

The Ópatans were concentrated in what is, today, Mexico; in the river valleys of the Serrana. They were thought by the Spaniards to be the most culturally advanced of the borderlands peoples. Among the Ópatan groups were the Eudeve and the Jova who spoke distinctly different dialects.

The Pimans were divided geographically into two groups; the Upper Pima and Lower Pima. Those in the Arizona-Sonora Borderlands were considered Upper Pimans. These Pimans were largely concentrated in the fertile river valleys of the Sonoran Desert. They lived in small settlements called *rancherías* by the Spanish. Among the Upper Pimans were two distinct groups; the Sobaipuri who farmed the Santa Cruz and San Pedro valleys and the Pápago (now called the Tohono O'Odam). The Pápagos were different from other Pimans in that they lived in the desert plains and followed a semi-nomadic lifestyle.

Native Peoples of the Spanish Colonial Northwest

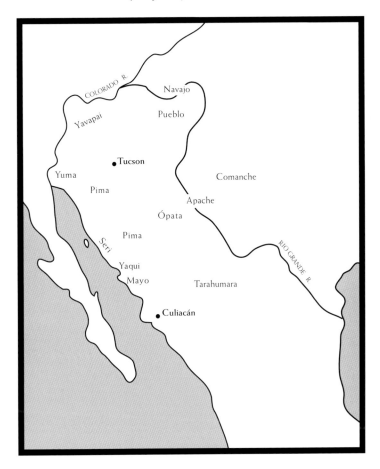

The most common of the Jesuit monograms found in early mission churches held the letters IHS and often incorporated a cross. The letters are the first three in Greek for Jesus. Both Jesuit and Franciscan symbolism are present in this relief carving on the facade of the mission church of San Xavier del Bac in the Santa Cruz Valley (Walter).

Chapter 3

Establishment and Spread
of the Missionary System

The Franciscans were the first of the religious orders to penetrate what is today the U.S. Southwest. Fray Marcos de Niza's role has already been mentioned. Other Franciscans accompanied him on Coronado's expedition. One of them, Fray Juan de Padilla, became the first missionary to be killed by Native Americans on what was ultimately to become U.S. soil.

Disappointment with the results of the Coronado mission led to a lull in exploration. In 1579, three Franciscan friars, accompanied by a small contingent of soldiers and Indians, entered what is now New Mexico. All three were murdered by local natives. The following year, Fray Bernardino Beltrán joined with Antonio de Espejo to extensively explore New Mexico and northern Arizona, setting the stage for the first settlements in that region.

There were three corridors followed by missionaries and settlers from the Mexican heartland into what is today the U.S. Southwest: a western corridor, bounded by the western slopes of the Sierra Madre Occidental to the east and the Sea of Cortez to the west which led into southern Arizona; a middle corridor which led from the Mexican Central Plateau into modern-day New Mexico and Northeastern Arizona; and an eastern corridor that led into Texas. The Franciscans primarily operated along the central and the eastern routes. The Jesuits were also active along the left flank of the middle corridor but made their most concerted advance in the west.

In 1598, a group of Franciscan friars accompanied Juan de Oñate through the middle corridor in an expedition that successfully colonized New Mexico. Missions were established in the New Mexico-Arizona region, but these were wiped out in 1680 by a major Indian Revolt. The Franciscans subsequently reestablished missions in New Mexico, but made no further effort to proselytize in Arizona due to an agreement, discussed below, which placed Sonora (and hence Arizona) within the Jesuit domain.

The Jesuits began their thrust northward through the western corridor in 1591, with the arrival of Padres Gonzalo de Tapia and Martin Pérez at a site on the Sinaloa River. The two established a mission near modern-day Culiacán. Tapia was killed three years later, but Pérez remained active until 1622. Meanwhile, other Jesuits arrived and, before the turn of the century, Indian peoples as far north as the Fuerte River Valley were being converted to Christianity.

The peoples north of the Fuerte were called the Mayo and the Yaqui. They occupied fertile river valleys of the same names. Undertaking their conversion

Corridors of Advance into the Borderlands

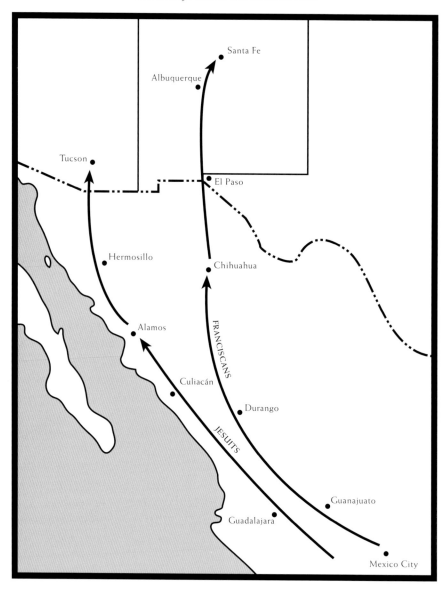

Depicted are the western and central corridors of advance used by the Jesuits and Franciscans.

was accomplished in close cooperation with Spanish civil authorities. Peace treaties were signed in 1609 and 1610. By 1614, spearheaded by the example of the Portuguese Jesuit Pedro Méndez, the Jesuits advanced to the Mayo River. By 1617, they were evangelizing along the Yaqui. The Jesuits persuaded the scattered Yaqui to consolidate their population at eight town sites where, in 1623, the first stone chapel was built in the centrally located town of Tórim.

Northward, beyond the land of the Yaqui, lay the inhospitable coastal territory of the Seri Indians and the fertile interior river valleys of the Pima and the Ópata. In 1627, Padre Méndez, who was now in his seventies, carried his pioneering effort to the southern Ópatas around the confluence of the Mátape, Moctezuma and middle Yaqui Rivers. Méndez was well-received, but some missionaries at other locations along the rim of the Ópata and lower Pima territories were not. Where native reluctance was encountered, it was overcome through a combination of Jesuit aggressiveness and Spanish military force. By 1636, the Jesuits had pushed beyond modern-day Hermosillo to establish a mission among the Ópata near the Sonora River at Ures.

By 1646, the Jesuits had advanced up four river valleys that stretched northward from central Sonora. They had reached Sinoquipe on the Sonora River, Nacámeri (today Rayón) on the San Miguel, Cumpas on the Moctezuma, and Huásabas on the Bavispe. The advance continued and, two years later, the forward trace of the Jesuit mission chain had reached to within 50 miles of today's U.S.-Mexican border.

Between 1645 and 1652, however, the efforts of the Jesuits and Franciscans became entangled. Sonora had just been separated from the province of Sinaloa. The first Sonoran governor, Don Pedro de Perea, preferred the Franciscans over the Jesuits and recruited a group of Franciscans to operate there. A heated competition ensued between the Jesuits and Franciscans, with the Jesuit hierarchy protesting the Franciscan intrusion all the way to Mexico City. The matter was not fully resolved until 1652 when the Franciscan superior in Mexico City ordered all of his friars out of northern Sonora.

By the 1670's, the Jesuit mission system in northeastern Sonora had spread among the Ópatas along the full lengths of the Moctezuma, Sonora, and Bavispe Rivers. Further to the west, in territories occupied by the Seri and the Upper Pima, the advance took place more slowly. The coast and interior plain north of the Mátape River were largely dry and barren. This region was occupied only sparsely, mostly by the Seri. The Seri were a semi-nomadic people who subsisted by fishing, hunting, and gathering wild plants. In terms of language and culture, they were very different from the other Indian peoples the Jesuits had encountered in the western corridor.

The earliest well-documented encounter between the Seri and the Spanish, somewhere west of Ures in 1662, took the form of a violent battle. Over time, the Seri would repeatedly show their willingness to fight for their interests. Some Seri proved receptive to change and to some measure of assimilation. Beginning in 1679, through the initiative of the Jesuit Juan Fernández a group of Seri accepted settlement at a mission site on the San Miguel River between Nacámeri and Ures. They would also be settled at other sites along the San Miguel. In 1688, the Jesuit Adam Gilg began a long period of service among them which bore some minor fruit. Only a small number of the Seri ever accepted mission life. Those that did would be later driven from their good farmland in the San

Miguel Valley by colonists.

North of the Seri, and most densely settled in the Magdalena and Altar River Valleys, were peoples called the Upper Pima. The Jesuit hierarchy chose Fr. Eusebio Kino to lead the way into this region which would become known as the Upper Pimería (*Pimería Alta*). Kino had already been in New Spain for six years, mostly working in Baja California. In 1687, he launched his initiative in northern Sonora. Over the following 24 years, it would carry him as far north as the Gila River in Arizona.

Kino established his base of operations at Dolores, about 15 miles north of Cucurpe on the San Miguel River. From there, he traveled northwest, into the Magdalena River Valley and established mission sites at San Ignacio and Ímuris. Over the course of the following eight years he established missions at Magdalena, Cocóspera, Caborca, and at the Altar River Valley sites of Oquitoa, Sáric, Tubutama, and Pitiquito.

Kino relied heavily on native lay people to help him. It wasn't until 1693 that he received any Jesuit assistants. While his helpers and Jesuit subordinates handled most of the actual construction and activities of his missions, Kino personally undertook further exploration. He traveled northward into the Santa Cruz and San Pedro River Valleys, onto soil that is today Arizona. In 1691 he laid the groundwork for missions at Tumacácori and Guévavi. In subsequent years, his travels took him north, as far as the Gila River, and west to the Colorado.

During this period, Kino was not alone in the Sonoran frontier. To the southwest, Fr. Gilg was working among the Seri. To Kino's east, Fr. Marcos de Loyola and others were working with the Ópata in territory being penetrated by the Apache.

Kino, however, is best known. He became immensely popular among the Pima and was well-received wherever he went. His style was pragmatic. His pattern was to create an anticipation of goodwill by bringing livestock, new plant varieties, and farming know-how with him to native agricultural settlements. Sometimes he did this well before establishing missions at given sites. His leadership was critical to both the development and subsequent maintenance of friendly relations between the Spanish and the Indians. Kino had his detractors. Among the Indians, these were mostly the spiritual leaders and medicine men who lost status in newly Christianized communities. Among the Spanish, these were mostly civil officials and entrepreneurs who resented the protection Kino provided the Indians from taxation and labor exploitation.

In 1695, Kino experienced a setback. A local uprising in the Altar Valley had led him to arrange a meeting between local colonial officials and natives. At the meeting, the Pima representatives were massacred, unleashing a violent native revolt. Before it ended, the missions at Tubutama, Caborca, Magdalena, and Ímuris were substantially destroyed. The missionary at Caborca was murdered. It would take Kino most of the rest of his life to recover the missionary ground he had lost.

While rebuilding, however, Kino continued to push northward along the Santa Cruz River Valley. In 1700, he established missions at Bac, near modern-day Tucson, and at Guévavi, further to the south. San Xavier del Bac was to become the northernmost of the Jesuit mission sites. As much as Kino would have liked, it was beyond his resources to establish missions further north along the Gila River or to the east in the San Pedro valley.

Until his death from natural causes in 1711, Kino continued to roam the *Pimería Alta*, providing personal leadership, documenting geography of terrain still new to the Spanish pioneers, and preaching to Indian peoples. After his death, progress in the *Pimería Alta* ground to a halt and some of his work was temporarily undone. The Santa Cruz missions were left without a single resident priest as new Jesuit manpower was largely diverted to the Baja California missions.

Beginning in the 1730's, fresh Jesuit resources were invested in the *Pimería Alta* and the mission system regained much of its vigor. By 1750, there were nine Jesuits serving among the Upper Pima and the missionary effort was progressing smoothly. However, the following year, things began to unravel for the Jesuits and, more generally, for the mission system of the Upper Pimería.

Two catastrophic events occurred. In 1751, the Pima carried out their second major revolt against Spanish rule, killing more than 100 Spaniards and two Jesuit missionaries. As in 1695, the uprising wrought considerable havoc on the mission system. Then, in 1767, before the Jesuits could complete rebuilding, their entire order was expelled from New Spain.

The Franciscans took over the bulk of the Jesuit missions and, for the period of the next 75 years, admirably applied themselves to the physical improvement of the missions they had inherited. They rebuilt or otherwise renovated most of the mission churches, creating structures more permanent and elaborate than those they had found. They also vigorously extended the mission system into *Alta California*.

While the physical dimension of the Franciscan accomplishment is clear, the social and spiritual effectiveness of their work has been debated. It is the view of at least some historians that, with the departure of the Jesuits, the vitality of the mission system began to wane. Edward Spicer, in his classic work *Cycles of Conquest*, judged the Franciscans to be generally less involved in Indian community life than the Jesuits. He saw the departure of the Jesuits as the beginning of the disintegration of the mission communities. The best efforts of the Franciscans were, in any case, blunted by a host of obstacles, most notably epidemics of contagious diseases, increasingly damaging Apache attacks, and cuts in resources and their authority over the Indians they served. These influences are discussed at further length later in the book.

This likeness of the Jesuit missionary Eusebio Kino is on a plaque located in the central plaza of the town of Ímuris, in the Magdalena Valley (Walter).

Chapter 4
The Missionaries
and Their Collaborators

The mission system spread through the efforts of a very diverse assortment of men dedicated to the propagation of Christianity. The Franciscan order had been founded by Francis of Assisi early in the thirteenth century. It had a long history of activity in Europe and elsewhere before becoming involved in the Americas. The Jesuit order's founding, on the other hand, actually post-dated the Spanish Conquest. The Society of Jesus was established in 1540 by Ignatius of Loyola. One of the Order's six original disciples, Francis Xavier, had proselytized in the Orient before meeting his untimely death there in 1552. Francis Xavier was the inspirational model for the Jesuit missionaries in New Spain. The Jesuits quickly gained a reputation there for courage, aggressiveness, and innovativeness in their work.

Some noted scholars, like Edward Spicer, have drawn a clear distinction between the general operating styles of the Jesuits and Franciscans. As previously mentioned, Spicer, in comparing the Franciscans of New Mexico to the Jesuits of Sonora, found the Jesuits to be more intimately involved with community affairs, more inclined to become proficient in the native languages, and less dependent on Spanish military protection. Some Jesuits of the period expressed apprehension that the Franciscan approach would alienate the Indians and hinder the missionary effort.

Others who have studied the history of the religious orders in the Americas make less of such distinctions. Even Spicer noted that different circumstances precipitated different approaches to evangelization among the Jesuits. Further, individual missionaries sometimes reacted to the challenges of their assignments in unique personality-driven ways. Some missionaries were appreciative of native culture and beloved by the people they served. Others were as much feared as respected for their stern, uncompromising dispositions.

We know much more about some of these earlier missionaries than others. Those who were prolific in writing reports and memoirs have provided us with the most complete portraits of themselves and others around them. In this category are people like: Andrés Pérez de Ribas, the first missionary to the Yaqui; Adam Gilg, pioneer among the Seri; Juan Nentvig and Ignaz Pfefferkorn, who worked among the Ópata and Pima, and the most renowned of all the Jesuits, Eusebio Kino, who worked mostly with the Pima.

We know that, initially, only Spaniards were authorized to serve in New Spain. But, we also know that during this early period, zealous European Jesuits

This statue of the pioneer Jesuit Bartolomé Castaño is located in the central plaza of the town of Baviácora, in the Sonora valley (Walter).

Portrait of Fray Francisco Gárces, first resident Franciscan missionary of San Xavier del Bac, located in the museum of Tumacácori National Historical Park (Walter).

from other countries found their way to the Americas and operated under Spanish aliases. Those in Sonora included the Flemings Giles Froidmont, alias Egidio Montefrío, and Van der Veken, alias Marcos del Río. Also in this category was the Irishman Michael Wadding, alias Miguel Godínez. Much of the most important missionary work was done by non-Spaniards, like the Germans Pfefferkorn and Sedelmayr, the Moravians Gilg and Kellner, and the Italian Kino.

It is clear that missionary work in the frontier placed very heavy demands on the priests who found themselves there. Some, like Kino and the Franciscan Fray Gárces seemed naturally suited for the rigors of the wilderness. Others like San Xavier del Bac's first resident, Francisco Gonzalvo, came and passed out of the system very quickly, victims of disease, stress, mysterious illnesses, or hostile Indian encounters. Some, like the Swiss Felipe Ségesser proved unsuitable, over time, for the rigors of frontline missions but served well in areas of lesser hardship. Those that survived and succeeded in their work played an invaluable role in the assimilation of the native peoples into the European-style society that was relentlessly spreading across the landscape of the Americas.

More will be said about specific missionaries and their contributions in the ensuing chapters as we focus on the development of specific mission chains. But little is known about some of them beyond the bare facts of where they were born and some of the places where they served.

From the perspective of assimilation, the natives of the Arizona-Sonora borderlands fared better in the northward expansion from the Mexican interior than did Indian peoples confronted with the westward expansion from the Atlantic seaboard. In Mexico today, there are few isolated Indian groups and relatively few individuals who consider themselves "pure" Indians. The degree of assimilation is, in significant measure, attributable to the socialization of native peoples by the missionaries.

Because of this book's perspective, i.e., the mission building process of the Jesuit and Franciscan orders, it risks creating the false impression that the missionaries acted in a vacuum or in a relatively passive countryside and that their success or failure was simply a function of circumstances, individual abilities, and, perhaps, the will of God. Thus, it is important to note that the relative success of missionaries was also significantly influenced by the attitudes and actions of Spanish colonial officials and local indigenous leaders.

As already noted, the missionary entrance into Sonora was largely enabled by peace treaties negotiated with the Mayo and Yaqui. In these instances, the captain-general of the Province of Sinaloa at the time, Don Diego Martínez de Hurdaide, was a key factor. The establishment of Sonora as a separate province and the introduction of Franciscans into that province shortly afterward were initiatives of Hurdaide's successor, Don Pedro de Perea. Frontier military leaders often worked very closely with the missionaries. Thus, Juan Mateo Mange supported Eusebio Kino, Juan Bautista de Anza (the elder) worked closely with José Augustín Campos, and Anza (the younger), commander of Tubac and

Above: Painting of Antonio de los Reyes, a Franciscan missionary who served at the Cucurpe mission and went on to become the first bishop of Sonora. This painting is displayed with those of subsequent Sonoran bishops in the first cathedral of the Sonoran Diocese, the Jesuit church of Nuestra Señora de la Asunción in Arizpe, Sonora (Walter).

Right: Statue of Juan Bautista de Anza, eighteenth century captain of the Presidio of Tubac in Arizona, stands in a park in downtown Hermosillo, the Sonoran state capital (Walter).

founder of the San Francisco Bay colony, collaborated productively with the first Franciscan missionary of San Xavier del Bac, Francisco Gárces.

Among the Indian population, leaders like Sisibotari of the Ópata and Coxi of the Upper Pima were crucial to the receptive attitudes that the Jesuits generally encountered. The Jesuits invariably relied on Christianized Indians that they took with them to help spread the mission system northward. A notable example cited by Schuetz-Miller and Fontana in a yet unpublished manuscript is that of a Lower Pima artisan, Francisco Monte, who accompanied Fr. Kino into the Upper Pimería. Monte, in addition to filling the roles of interpreter, catechist, and mission supervisor, was a talented painter whose decorative work helped brighten mission interiors. Such natives also acted as escorts and advisors and provided a skilled labor cadre for the building of new missions and establishing the organizations that constituted the support structure for the economic and social activity of the missions.

Local secular leaders also kept the Christian faith alive and mission buildings in working order in the absence of resident missionaries. Such leaders were especially crucial to the survival of the Catholic temples in the transitional periods between, first, the Jesuits and Franciscans and, then, between the Franciscans and the diocesan clergy.

The rich decorative detail of the facade of San Pedro y San Pablo de Tubutama (above) stands in sharp contrast to the simplicity of the face of San Diego de Pitiquito (right). Both churches are located in the Altar Valley (Grabas).

Chapter 5
The Churches
Construction And Life Cycles
C

The building of a church as a center of religious instruction, prayer, and worship, was among the highest priorities of missionaries wherever they went. The form that these mission churches (or temples, as they are sometimes called) took was largely a function of the local environment and circumstances at the time of a missionary's arrival at a given location. As circumstances permitted, the nature of the temple became more elaborate. The architects of many of the more permanent churches were often master builders from central Mexico. The physical work of construction and reconstruction was most often carried out by regional or local artisans.

The churches of the Jesuits and Franciscans were battered by a variety of destructive forces over their lifetimes. Each temple experienced its own life cycle. Decline sometimes led to destruction. In other cases it led to renewal. What we see today is invariably a mix of elements of different periods of construction that is, in most cases, eye-pleasing.

Unfortunately, available records do not completely track the changing fortunes of most of the mission churches. Even accounts that exist can be deceiving. For example, Buford Pickens, editor of *The Missions of Northern Sonora*, noted the difficulty in interpreting historical reports relating to the destruction of missions and the building of new churches on their sites. His book, based on an exhaustive 1935 field documentation study, concludes that "new" churches often incorporated substantial construction from the "destroyed" churches they replaced. To what extent this was the case in a given instance is often difficult to determine.

In its earliest and simplest form, the center of worship was a basic shelter made of the same materials the local Indians used for their homes. At times it took the form of a ramada made of poles and bent rods covered with bundles of brush and overlaid with mud. This might graduate to a sturdier fully-enclosed structure of closely-spaced wood poles, sealed with mud or clay, and overlaid with mud and grass. Whatever the initial form of the shelter, the missionaries were inclined to build, at the earliest practical time, an enduring structure that would attractively serve as a focus for Christian community life.

There was no standard design or architecture for the missions, although churchbuilders were obviously influenced by the prevailing European styles of their period. Styles in Spain underwent changes during the mission building period from the Gothic-Mooresque style known as Plateresque, to Baroque and,

Post-and-Lintel Construction

The mission church of San Antonio Paduano de Oquitoa in the Altar Valley provides the best example of post-and-lintel construction in the Arizona-Sonora Borderlands. Here, heavy pieces of mesquite wood, positioned horizontally, bridge doorway and window openings and sustain the weight of overhead wall material (Grabas).

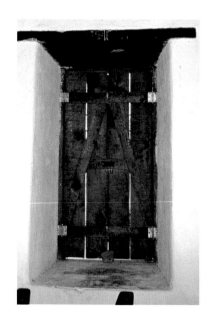

later, Churrigueresque. The appearance that a temple assumed was largely a matter of the taste of the missionary onsite or that of its chief professional builder and resources available for construction. Indigenous influences also crept into construction through the initiatives of Native American artisans, especially in the area of decorative detail.

Regardless of the builder's taste, ambitions were tempered by the willingness and skills of the Indian labor available. At times the thirst for the missionary's arrival was so strong that indigenous communities built churches on their own initiative to stimulate the coming. More commonly, however, the missionary would have to motivate the local people toward the task, do his own planning, and supervise his church's construction.

The size of a European-style church and the use of unfamiliar construction materials and techniques presented a significant challenge to indigenous peoples whose dwellings were characteristically small, basic, and relatively perishable. Among the first tasks a missionary faced at a given location was to create a framework for social and economic development that included a labor organization with work supervisors, adobe-makers, and laborers of other discrete skills to include carpentry, stonecutting, and blacksmithing. Commonly, missionaries like Kino brought a trained cadre of native builders with them from previously Christianized communities. This cadre shared building skills and guided, at least initially, the process of mission construction.

Out of practical necessity, missions were built mostly from materials available near the construction site. Walls of early churches were commonly of sun-dried adobe brick and local stone. Early adobe walls were covered with a thin, mud plaster and then coated with whitewash. Later, a cement mortar was developed as a protective sealant to be spread on exterior adobe walls.

Structural systems of churches were of either the post-and-lintel variety or the arch-and-pier system. Initially, the post-and-lintel system, employing a flat roof, predominated. The use of adobe dictated the building of thick walls because of the poor load bearing capacity of the material. In the case of the early churches, the interior width of a church's main hall (its nave) was limited by the length and strength of beams (called *vigas*) that could be hewn from available trees as well as the capacity of the walls to accept the overhead stress that the roof created.

With time, the use of fired clay brick was incorporated into the building of walls, wall facings, piers, vaulted ceilings, and domes. Exterior brick facing was commonly covered with stucco, while interior facing was covered with a lime plaster. Plaster was also employed to create decorative wall detail. Wall blocks were bonded with mud or lime mortar, depending on the period of construction and the nature of the block.

In addition to roof spans, wood was used for lintels, doors, windows, jambs, and sills. Mesquite and, to a lesser degree, pine were the woods most commonly employed for beams. Wooden corbels (beam supports) were often extended from

Ceiling Construction

The above example, at San Antonio Paduano de Oquitoa, illustrates the common early technique of using saguaro ribs and cane as decking to fill the space between ceiling support beams. In the below example, at the church of San Lorenzo de Huépac in the Sonora Valley, wood planking is employed between closely spaced support beams. Corbels are used to help support the mesquite beams in both cases. The hand-carved corbels of the Huépac church are unique in extending more than one-third of the width of the hall. They are also the most elaborate corbels to be found in missions along the U.S.-Mexican Borderlands (Grabas).

Interior Design

The central aisle (or nave) of an early frontier mission church was often narrow because of the unavailability of timber that could span a wider space. Some churches were designed with wings (called transepts) which were equipped with their own altars. Interior walls were most commonly white-washed and painted with dados and designs inspired by textile patterns or in imitation of fine but unavailable building materials such as ceramic tiles and marble, or figures and scenes drawn from the bible used for teaching purposes.

This interior view is of Nuestra Señora de la Asunción de Arizpe in the Sonora Valley. The unusually high ceiling is distinguished by hand-carved corbels. The pine vigas supporting the ceiling have been dated by tree ring analysis to the mid-eighteenth century. The church is divided into bays with the use of pilasters and arches. Bay ceilings give the impression of sloping contrastingly toward alternate side walls (Grabas).

The area behind an altar was commonly decorated with an elaborate back-drop called a retablo. The retablo was composed of a number of elements. Much of the design was created from carved wood that was, afterwards, coated with a mixture of plaster of paris or gypsum prepared with glue (called gesso) and, then, gilded. Retablos usually incorporated oil painted canvasses and provided one or more niches or pedestals for images. Ornate retablos were made in the workshops of central Mexico and shipped to the frontier to be reassembled.

This chapel in the church of San Miguel Arcángel de Oposura in the Moctezuma Valley is seen through its wooden archway from the nave. Its ornate retablo is kept devoid of moveable furnishings except during special annual activities of the Easter Holy Week (Grabas).

This retablo is in the right transept of the church of Nuestra Señora de la
Asunción de Arizpe. The eighteenth century gilt-framed oil paintings
which surround the statue of Mary (as our Lady of Loreto) were recently
restored. A similar retablo is located in the left transept, with a statue of
St. Ignatius de Loyola in the central niche (Walter).

Mission Church Belfries

Wall-type belfry at San Lorenzo de Huépac (Grabas).

Two-tiered belltower of the church of San Xavier del Bac (Walter).

View from south arch of belltower toward village square, Nuestro Padre San Ignacio de Cabórica (Grabas).

This bell hangs from a temporary rack of a church that was never completed. It is part of the ruins of the church of Los Santos Reyes de Cucurpe in the San Miguel Valley (Grabas).

Two-tiered belltower and domed passageway to roof of the church of Nuestro Padre San Ignacio de Cabórica in the Magdalena Valley (Grabas).

This view is from inside the belltower of the church of San Pedro y San Pablo de Tubutama.

the interior walls under the beams to increase their load bearing capacity. Saguaro ribs, Ocotillo and cane were commonly used to provide for the finished flat interior roofing. Also used were wooden laths, and peeled poles. These materials were laid side-by-side, across and at right-angle to the ceiling beams or set in patterns, e.g., herringbone. Later, many temples were built with vaulted roofs of brick or stone, covered with plaster.

Domes constructed of brick were also incorporated into the roofs of many churches. Walls were often strengthened with exterior buttresses to compensate for the stress created by vaulted roof and dome construction.

Decoration on the exterior walls of churches was largely limited to the facade. The amount of decoration here varied considerably. In the case of some of the lesser important visitas, like Pitiquito and Rayón, decoration was limited to the immediate area surrounding the entranceway. At the other end of the spectrum, San Xavier del Bac and Tubutama were given elaborate ornamentation that covered virtually the entire facade between belltowers.

Most of the churches of the region had belltowers. Bells signaled important events of mission community life. The majority of the church belltowers were two stories and capped by a dome. There were, however, plenty of exceptions to this style to include one-story towers and the wall-type belfry. The latter was constructed as an extension of the wall above the roof line with arched openings to hold the bells.

Floor plans varied. They included that of the simple hall church, with a long, narrow single aisle shape and those built following a cruciform-style plan.

Most religious statuary was produced in central Mexico by teams of craftsmen. First, the figure was carved from a wood, such as oak or cottonwood, by a master sculpturer. Then, a thin coat of plaster (called gesso) was applied to the statue's surface. Finally, other detail work, such as skin pigmentation and the painting of clothing and gold leaf ornamentation, was accomplished.

While the majority of statues were of solid construction and made solely for display, others were made for both display and processional purposes. Most notable in this latter category are the thematic figures of Christ and Mary, in the respective roles of "Jesus of Nazarene" and "Our Lady of Sorrows." The dual purpose statues were only partially carved. They were built of a combination of materials to make them lighter and, in the case of Christ, to provide moveable joints. To reduce weight, light woods and materials such as corn stalks were used for parts of the form covered by clothing. Moveable wood joints were connected with leather strips. Where the joints were to be left uncovered by clothing, plaster was sometimes feathered around the strips to create a natural appearance.

Some statuary, probably intended mostly for exterior niches, was made out of stone rubble and stucco, using a molded form. They were then finished with plaster. Examples of this construction can still be seen at the mission church of San Xavier del Bac.

As already noted, all the historic churches found today at the sites of the

This beautiful crucifix, carved in wood and painted black, dominates the main altar of the church of San Pedro de Aconchi in the Sonora Valley (Upper photo by Grabas; lower photo by Walter). Images of Christ in black, found from place to place in Latin America, are traditionally associated with a religious devotion that encompasses a belief in healing waters. Another historic "Black Christ" crucifix, removed from the Tucson Presidio by Mexican soldiers after the Gadsden Purchase of 1853, is now in the church of Señor San José de Ímuris in the Magdalena valley. This latter crucifix was recently repainted polychrome.

This highly detailed crucifix is along an interior side wall of the church of San Luis Gonzaga de Bacadéhuachi. The thin plaster coating over the face is worn away in places to expose the carved wood base (Walter).

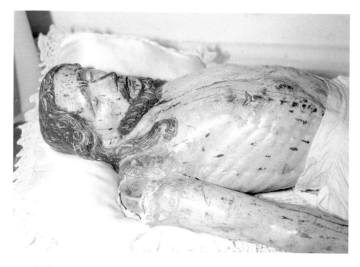

This reclining crucified Christ is located in the church of San Ignacio de Cabórica. Stretched leather has been used to encase a shoulder socket that provides for a moveable wooden joint (Grabas).

This statue of St. Francis of Assisi is in the museum at the Tumacácori National Historical Park, located at the site of the mission of San José de Tumacácori (Walter).

Opposite: The most popular manifestation of Christ's mother found in Mexico is that of Our Lady of Guadalupe. The Mexican devotion springs from an apparition first witnessed by an indigenous peasant on a hilltop near Mexico City in the sixteenth century and from subsequent miracles attributed to her. The icon of Our Lady of Guadalupe is richly laden with symbolism of pre-Columbian Native American culture. In borderlands churches she is depicted more often in painted portraits than in statuary. This portrait is located in the church of San Antonio Paduano de Oquitoa (Walter).

Saint Joseph, as an essential element of the Holy Family, is a popular character in the statuary found in the frontier mission system. Such statues were all originally accompanied by a statue of the infant Jesus. However, in the case of the above figure, located in the church of San Diego de Pitiquito in the Altar valley, the statue of Jesus is missing (Grabas). The lower statue is in the church of San Luis de Gonzaga de Bacadéhuachi (Walter).

This statue of Santa Bárbara is located in a facade niche of the church of San Xavier del Bac, near Tucson (Walter).

This statue, located in an interior wall niche of the church of San Ignacio de Cabórica, is considered by the local populace to be Santa Lucía. However, it was constructed as an image of Mary Magdalene and is believed to have been taken from the visita in Magdalena, Sonora. As indicated by the many little objects (called milagros) placed around it, this statue is venerated. Prayers are offered to Santa Lucía for cures to eye problems (Grabas).

This statue of St. Francis Xavier is in the church of San Xavier del Bac. Francis was a colleague of Ignatius de Loyola and one of the original Jesuits. He served and died in Asia. Recognized as the greatest of their early missionaries, he became the role model of the frontier Jesuits. His likeness is found throughout the Jesuit mission chain and is most commonly depicted as here, in a funeral bier. Highly venerated to this day, he is credited with countless miracles of healing (Walter)

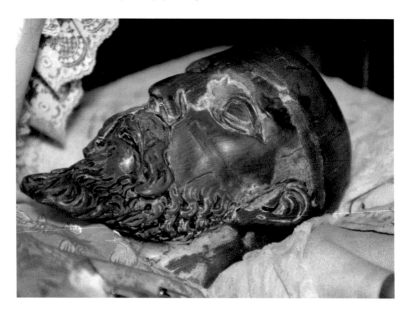

original Jesuit missions have been altered by the circumstances of time, some more so than others. Among these are some active churches which are essentially Jesuit structures that have substantially retained their original character. However, most of them are working churches that have been reconstructed since the Jesuit period. Of these, the majority were built (or significantly rebuilt) by the Franciscans. Others are newer nineteenth century structures built after the missionary period by diocesan initiative.

In another category are the mission churches that have fallen into ruin. Some, for example at Guévavi, are only marked by wall fragments and mounds. Others, such as at Cocóspera and Baviácora are considerably more intact and retain some traces of their former glory.

Beyond the effects of weathering, the circumstances of decline and, in some cases, restoration are diverse. Human historical events influenced the physical condition of all of these buildings to varying degrees. Localized events have affected some but not others. There are also the important variables of whether a church has enjoyed the continued presence of a served population and, where it has, the degree of a congregation's dedication to the maintenance of its temple of worship. Some missions were simply abandoned and left without caretakers. Others, located within stable, enduring communities, were preserved in ways that are practical, but not necessarily faithful to the original appearance of these buildings.

The most catastrophically damaging of human activities to mission churches was Indian attack. Such attacks roughly fell into two categories; attacks by revolting missionized peoples and attacks by non-missionized marauding bands. Most notable in the former category were the Pima Revolts of 1695 and 1751 which affected most directly the missions of the Santa Cruz, Altar, and Magdalena Valleys. Most notable in the latter category were recurring Apache attacks, beginning in the late seventeenth century and continuing well into the nineteenth century. These had their greatest impact on the missions along the northern rim of the frontier.

The negative impacts of marauding Indians and infectious disease epidemics on mission populations undercut the support of many mission stations. While the missionaries were the managers and leaders, the Christianized Indians were the very life blood of the mission system. In the eighteenth century, missionized Indian populations declined considerably.

As the mission system extended itself further to the north, the supply of missionaries over the full area of the system became attenuated. The Jesuits were reluctant to turn over any part of their missionary field to secular authority or to other mission societies and so, even while their overall numbers within the borderlands somewhat increased over the period of their presence, the quality of the service to populations at specific mission stations sometimes declined. There was often a greater Indian demand for missionaries at potential as well as established mission sites than the system could satisfy.

Expansion northward into Arizona in the early eighteenth century was also slowed by the Jesuit hierarchy. A decision was made to prioritize the assignment of new missionary manpower away from Sonora and toward Baja California.

Limitations imposed by civil government impacted on the vitality of missionary activity in a much more telling and lasting way. Here, the motive was to emasculate the missionary orders by eliminating their local economic base and to, ultimately, replace them entirely. Over time, religious functions were to be transferred to a religious bureaucracy more attuned to the needs of civil government and a population which had become "fully Christianized." The process of turning over religious functions from missionary orders to a diocesan bureaucracy and mission churches to parish priests accountable to the diocese was called "secularization."

As previously noted, the first major blow by civil authority was struck by the Spanish king when, in 1767, he executed a plan that expelled the Jesuits from his colonies. This plan also contained provisions to generally reduce the influence of all mission societies in New Spain by expropriating their financial holdings and legally severing obligatory ties between missionized Indians and the missions. The latter two measures were substantively reversed after two years, but by this time a good deal of damage had already been done. Further, similar measures would be instituted by a newly independent Mexican government in the 1820's.

The expulsion of the Jesuits from New Spain created an immediate and unexpected vacuum in the Borderlands and an immense challenge for the Franciscans. Even where they moved quickly to replace the Jesuits, the Franciscans could not effectively assume control over every mission left leaderless. Further, the Jesuit style was somewhat different from that of the Franciscans and this, at times, presented an obstacle in establishing relationships between the missionary and his newly-adopted clientele.

After independence, the Mexican government expelled all peninsula-born Spaniards. The majority of Franciscan missionaries in the Sonoran-Arizona frontier fell into that category and could not be replaced. Then, in 1834, the Mexican government dealt the death blow to the mission system by publishing a decree that secularized all missions on Mexican soil.

The missionary's role was seen to have outlived its practical usefulness and to have become counterproductive to economic development. At the local level, missions had come to compete with farmers and ranchers in the sale of their products. Further, and especially in the case of the Jesuits, the missionary societies had sought to shelter the Indians from exploitive labor practices and taxation.

The quality of the lay leadership and the degree of local commitment to the survival of the mission system were crucial factors in determining how well the transition from Jesuit to Franciscan leadership progressed. These factors were also crucial to the effectiveness of the later transition from Franciscan leadership to diocesan control. The Diocese of Sonora was created in 1779. Its hierarchy was generally less zealous in its attention to the overall needs of the populations of frontier communities than were the missionary orders. The organization of a secular clergy took time to develop. It never did effectively evolve in the northern reaches of the *Pimería Alta* in the colonial period.

Throughout the nineteenth century, the Catholic Church, as a social institution, was part of the exploitive power elite that governed Mexico. The vast majority of the populace lived in poverty. Resentment among the masses generated anger that exploded in violent revolution in the first decade of the twentieth century. The Church bore a full share of the brunt of the revolutionary fury and the secularized mission churches suffered as targets of hostility along with other symbols of institutional oppression. The nature of attacks on churches ranged from mindless vandalism to the theft of valuables to finance warfighting.

The anti-clerical sentiment that characterized the revolution was transmitted to the post-revolutionary Constitution of 1917 which severely limited the role of the Church in Mexican society. The implementation of these constitutional provisions by Plutarco Elías Calles during his presidency in the 1920's led to a violent social convulsion. Militant Catholic backlash was answered by suppressive government countermeasures. Some churches were closed or converted to secular functions in ways that physically erased religious features. Sacred objects were removed from church interiors, some never to be returned. Planned construction and renovations were left on hold.

These times passed. Mexican society came to a relative peace with its Catholic heritage. But, the disruption in the care of many of the temples resulted in irreplaceable losses. Fortunately, devotees often removed and secured valuables until circumstances were more propitious for their return. Some revered objects lost, like the venerated statue of San Francisco Xavier in the chapel at Magdalena, were replaced by copies which again serve the religious needs of the faithful. Further, many of the churches which suffered from neglect or animosity in the early decades of the twentieth century have since benefited from a reinvestment of material resources and renovation.

San Miguel Arcángel de Ures

The exterior of this eighteenth century Franciscan church is perhaps most notable for its clean lines and the flying buttresses that extend from the right side wall. The neo-baroque facade is relatively plain. A contemporary statue of the church's patron, St. Michael, is located on the skyline of the facade between the two belltowers (Grabas).

La Purisima Concepción de Baviácora

The seventeenth century Jesuit church (on the left) is now in ruin. Its replacement stands alongside it. The older church was reconstructed a number of times before being abandoned, and its unusual Moorish facade and central minaret-style tower are not part of its original design. A statue in the plaza in front of the church honors Bartolomé Castaño as "Padre Indio" for his work among the Ópata in the Sonora Valley (Grabas).

Chapter 6
Sonora River Valley
&

The Sonora Valley missions are linked by a single road paralleling the river's course. The road, numbered #089 between Mazacahui and Cananea, is similar to rural roads in the United States. It is paved, has two lanes (one for each direction of traffic), and has an occasional pull-off for emergency roadside stops.

The northern valley area is most quickly reached from Arizona by traveling Mexican Federal Highway #2 to Cananea, Sonora from Douglas or Naco, Arizona. Highway #2 is also characteristically similar to rural U.S. routes. At the outskirts of Cananea, the way to Highway #089 is marked by directional signs to Arizpe. Highway #2 can also be accessed from Nogales, Arizona by traveling south on Mexican Federal Highway #15 to Ímuris, Sonora. Highway #15 is the best road in Sonora. It offers two lanes for each direction of traffic, with a median separating direction of flow in most places. The southern valley area can be reached via Highways #2 and #089 or about as quickly by traveling Highway #15 south to the Ures, Sonora exit. From Ures, follow Highway #14 northeast to Mazacahui.

In some cases the churches (or at least their belfries) are visible from Highway #089 as it passes by or through the communities it connects. In other cases, the traveler is compelled to ask directions or wander around town to find the church.

The Sonora River Valley is generally believed to be the route taken northward by Niza and Coronado in the early sixteenth century. Niza made no effort to establish missions at the time. It was not until roughly 100 years later that the Jesuits reached this area and set about the task.

Jesuits began working in the Sonora Valley in the mid-1630's. The Mexican-born Padre Lorenzo de Cárdenas, was apparently the first. He was joined by Pedro Pantoja and Bartolomé Castaño. Pantoja and Castaño are credited with establishing mission sites at Baviácora, Aconchi, Banámichi, and Sinoquipe. Castaño, a Portuguese Jesuit, evidently made the strongest impression of the three, although Pantoja stayed longer. Today, Castaño remains the best locally known of the early missionaries. He was, purportedly, a popular dark-skinned man with an "easy intimacy" who was a good musician and talented in languages.

The spread of the missionary system in the Sonora Valley was rapid. It might have been even faster if Castaño had been left there. The reason for his sudden removal is unclear. However, based on the limited information available, Spicer supposed that Castaño's superiors may have been uncomfortable with his style and his closeness to the Indians.

In 1648, the Mexican-born Jesuit Gerónimo de Canal extended the Jesuit mission chain north along the Sonora River, establishing missions in Arizpe and

Above: San Lorenzo de Huépac

Local residents consider this to be the early Jesuit church in place in 1679. The building has undergone reconstruction over time, to include exterior stylistic changes (Grabas).

Right: San Pedro de Aconchi

This seventeenth century Jesuit church has an unusual frontal appearance, largely due to two massive octagonal towers that dominate the facade, extending from beyond the church's front corners. The facade itself is very simple except for an intricate Franciscan design in bas-relief above the door (Grabas).

beyond. It had taken the Jesuits only 12 years to establish a line of missions and visitas northward from Ures, in central Sonora, to the settlement of Bacoachi, located less than 50 miles south of what is today the U.S. border.

Each of the important mission sites in the Sonora Valley are featured separately in the following pages, essentially in the sequence they were established.

Ures

Ures was the early point of departure for missionaries moving into the Sonora Valley. It was an important early colonial settlement in Sonora and, in the nineteenth century, it was Sonora's capital for about 30 years.

The mission in Ures was founded by Jesuit Francisco Paris in 1636. The original church was constructed in the 1640's. This church deteriorated over time to the point that in 1775 the Franciscan resident missionary, Esteban Salazar, built a new church. Salazar's church is the one that exists today.

Baviácora

This was the first early mission settlement north of Ures. Baviácora became Pantoja's *cabecera* and a church was built between 1638-39. Pantoja was given the title "Superior of the Northern Missions". He stayed at Baviácora until replaced by Fr. Antonio de Heredía in 1658. Subsequently, Baviácora served as residence for a variety of missionaries some of whom would go on to serve in new missions along the frontier as it spread northward. Its last resident missionary was Fr. Nicolás Perera, who arrived in 1750. In 1761, Perera moved on to reestablish the *cabecera* at Aconchi.

Aconchi

The Aconchi mission was founded between 1638 and 1639 by Bartolomé Castaño and served as his residence until 1645. Afterwards it became a *visita* of Baviácora. It became a *cabecera* again in 1678, with the arrival of Fr. Juan Fernández. It maintained that status till the turn of the century when it became a *visita* again until the arrival of Perera in 1761. Perera remained there until the Jesuit expulsion. As in the case of Baviácora, the church here was officially secularized shortly after the expulsion of the Jesuits, although the congregation continued to be served periodically by Franciscans. The church at Aconchi is the repository of a regionally famous colonial-era carving known as *"El Cristo Negro"*.

Interior view of the nave of San Lorenzo de Huépac (Walter).

Detail of one of the original stone column facings, inside the church near the main entrance (Walter).

Huépac

Huépac was apparently given little attention by Castaño and Pantoja on the way to Banámichi. Gerónimo de Canal established his *cabecera* there in 1646 and began building a church soon after. Canal stayed there till he died in 1662. A few years later, the Irish Jesuit Juan Muñoz de Burgos arrived and stayed till the end of the century. Burgos was followed by Antonio Leal (previously at Arizpe) and, then, by José Toral who invested a great deal of energy in improving the appearance and physical condition of all the churches within his jurisdiction. During his period of service, Toral moved his *cabecera* to Banámichi and Huépac became a *visita*.

The overall interior appearance of the church at Huépac is especially impressive among those in this mission chain. It is distinguished by a well-preserved beautiful wood ceiling. Handsomely carved stone pillars stand near the entrance. The original door is no longer used but set in place. Colonial-era religious figures are displayed throughout the nave.

Banámichi

Castaño and Pantoja built the first chapel in Banámichi in 1639. Governor Perea established his civil headquarters here and used Banámichi as a staging area for Franciscans. In 1646, the Jesuits reestablished their presence, first, with a *visita* and, later, under José Toral, with a *cabecera*. After Toral died in 1764, he was replaced by Fr. Francisco Javier Villaroya who remained the resident until the Jesuit expulsion.

Sinoquipe

The mission site at Sinoquipe was established in 1639 by Padres Pantoja and Castaño as a *visita* of Huépac. The first mission church was built by Padre Canal in 1653.

Arizpe

The town of Arizpe is at the junction of the Sonora and Bacanuche rivers. It was briefly served, initially, by the Franciscan Fray Juan Suarez, the leader of the Franciscans that Pedro de Perea brought to Banámichi. The Jesuit mission site of Nuestra Señora de la Asunción de Arizpe was established by Gerónimo de Canal in 1648.

The first resident Jesuit, the Sardinian-born Fr. Felipe Esgrecho, arrived in 1650. Upon his death in 1692, he was replaced by Fr. Antonio Leal. Two years later, the residence was assumed by the Mexican-born Fr. Francisco Javier Mora

San Lorenzo de Huépac

The original church door, no longer in use but kept for display against an interior wall near the church entrance (Walter).

Nuestra Señora de los Remedios de Banámichi

This church is believed to have been built in 1678, although the belltower and facade are of newer construction (Grabas).

This partially reconstructed arch is emplaced as a gateway to the yard surrounding the old Banámichi church and is from the main portal of the church's early facade. The detail of the arch is unusual in its incorporation of Native American symbolism (Walter).

Nuestra Señora de los Remedios de Banámichi

A view of the sanctuary. Two carved stone pier facings decorate the arch that frames the sanctuary's opening. These pier facings are among the few traces of antiquity found in the church's simply decorated and furnished interior (Grabas).

The church cemetery overlooking the village of Sinoquipe, with the church belltower to the rear (Walter).

Nuestro Padre San Ignacio de Sinoquipe

Right: This belltower is all that remains of the original Jesuit church. The tower has been refaced at the expense of its original appearance to protect it from the effects of the weather. The contemporary detached building to its rear is the present church (Grabas).

Nuestra Señora de la Asunción de Arizpe

*An unusual feature of the church is its unplastered stone and fired brick face.
The facade is organized in three horizontal decorative zones (architecturally
known as registers). Four pilasters run the full height of the facade but are
segmented by the lintels which separate the registers. There are empty wall
niches in each register and a considerable amount of symbolism that surrounds
a circular window at the center of the middle register. The symbolism includes
the nails of the passion and a medallion with Christ's monogram. The name of
Carlos Rojas with the date of 1756 is inscribed below these design features.
Today, the skyline of the facade is completely flat. It was originally finished
with a cornice topped with three pedestals of which the middle one would have
supported a cross (Walter).*

*Opposite: The main portal and surrounding features of the facade of the church of Nuestra Señora de la
Asunción de Arizpe (Walter).*

This altar and accompanying statuary in the old Arizpe church overwatch the remains of a colonial-era frontier captain displayed in a rail protected glass-top sarcophagus. While the uniformed skeleton (in an open wood coffin) is identified as Captain Juan Bautista de Anza, scholars have concluded that it is probably that of a contemporary, Manuel de Echeagary. Anza's remains are probably still buried under a side chapel of the church (Walter).

Right: San Miguel de Bacoachi

This old church is believed by the local residents to be an early Jesuit structure. The modern brick facade tends to create the impression that it is newer (Grabas).

who remained there until his death in 1720. During his time at Arizpe, Mora became an outspoken critic of Eusebio Kino. After Mora's departure, the mission was mostly run by the Mexican-born Fr. Carlos Rojas who remained there until the Jesuit expulsion. A single Franciscan, Juan Domínguez, served there before the church was secularized.

The church was built over a period of years beginning in the 1720's or a little earlier. It was finished around 1756 with significant reconstruction that enlarged it and raised its height, modified the facade, and provided the current belltower. The detached belltower is an unusual feature for frontier mission churches. There is an outside crosswalk from the tower to the main structure's choir loft. The belltower was not capped until sometime after 1879. A sketch made in that year shows a damaged structure on the opposing side of the church which may have been a second belltower.

Juan Bautista de Anza, the frontier captain of Tubac who led the group that founded the first settlement of San Francisco (California) in 1775, was married in this church. A skeleton purported to be his is enshrined for viewing in a glass-topped floor vault inside the nave.

In 1776, Arizpe was made capital of the PROVINCIAS INTERNAS, a political territory which included virtually all of what is today Northern Mexico and the U.S. Southwest. It also became the seat of the first Catholic Diocese of Sonora. Its church became the first diocesan cathedral. After Mexico achieved independence from Spain, Arizpe served, intermittently, as the capital of Sonora. However, it declined considerably in importance during the first half of the nineteenth century and is, today, essentially a quaint farming community.

Bacoachi

Bacoachi is about 30 miles north of Arizpe. Through the colonial period, it was frequently at the point of contact between the Spanish and marauding Apaches. Like Arizpe, it was at first briefly served by Franciscans and, then, incorporated into the Jesuit system by Canal. The first church here was built by 1678.

This doorway is to a chapel that stands amidst the ruins of the church of Los Santos Reyes de Cucurpe in the San Miguel Valley. This simple chapel, once part of the church, continues to serve the neighborhood as a place of worship today (Richards).

Chapter 7
San Miguel River Valley
℃

The northern most of the San Miguel valley missions sites, Cucurpe, is best reached from Magdalena. Take the local toll-free road into Magdalena. This becomes the main north-south street through town. On the south side of town, turn east onto Calle Kino Oriente. This turn is just north of a small park with a free-standing clock tower, on the east side of the main street. Continue on Calle Kino out of town. The distance to Cucurpe is about 30 miles. While a dirt road connects Cucurpe to the more southerly San Miguel valley mission sites, it is very poor. Don't take it. Los Ángeles and Horcasitas are best reached from the Federal Highway #15 tollbooth bypass north of Hermosillo. At the north edge of the town of Pesqueira, at a sharp road bend just east of the railroad crossing, take a dirt road traveling east. Continue past the ruins of an old mill complex. At an intersection shortly beyond, take a left turn onto another dirt road that leads generally north to Los Ángeles and Horcasitas. Rayón and Opodepe are best reached from a dirt road that travels northwest out of Ures. This road is on the south side of town and is marked by a directional sign.

The Jesuits arrived in the San Miguel Valley in the 1630's. They were amicably received by the native Eudeve and Pima inhabitants. The Eudeve, who were there in the largest numbers, were a branch of the Ópata people. Most of the Eudeve lived farther south in the valleys of the middle Yaqui, Mátape, and lower Moctezuma.

For awhile in the 1640's, the Jesuits were compelled to share the missionary effort in the San Miguel Valley with the Franciscans who were based in the northern part of the valley at Cucurpe. However, by 1652, the Franciscans were gone.

Beginning in 1679, at the initiative of the Jesuit Fr. Juan Fernández, several hundred Seri were settled at a mission site on the lower San Miguel Valley called Santa Maria de Pópulo. Fr. Adam Gilg took over this site in 1688. Gilg stayed for 16 years and settled other Seri at Pópulo. He also established Seri populations in the vicinity of the extant settlement of Nacámeri (today Rayón) and at another site south of Pópulo that was named Los Ángeles. Gilg was followed, first, by Fr. Miguel Almanza and, then, Nicolás Perera. Perera worked among the Seri in the area for at least 15 years and was, by some accounts, the most popular of the missionaries to serve them.

After the Franciscan departure from Cucurpe the Jesuits established a mission there. Padre Kino extended the Jesuit system even further from that location along the San Miguel in 1687, establishing the mission of Dolores at the location of the Indian village of Cósari, 15 miles upriver from Cucurpe. Dolores became Kino's headquarters for the ensuing 24 years.

Nuestra Señora del Rosario de Nacámeri (Rayón)

The original church, built beginning in 1678, was in ruins by 1772. The present church is apparently on the site of the first church and may incorporate the foundations and walls of that building. The most distinguishing feature of the existing structure is its two-tiered belfry, with a bell in each of the three arches of the lower tier (Grabas).

In 1748, The capital of Sonora was moved to the lower San Miguel River Valley, south of Pópulo, to a place named Horcasitas. The following year a presidio was also established there. It was during this time that the San Miguel River was given its name, and the settlement at the site of the new presidio became San Miguel de Horcasitas. In 1750, the governor of Sonora, Diego Parrilla, began expropriating the lands of the Seri and Pima around Pópula and redistributing them to Spanish settlers. The Seri revolted and, during a period of warfare lasting several years, they were permanently driven from the area. Horcasitas remained the capital of Sonora for roughly three decades. Afterwards, the seat of government was transferred to Arizpe and the San Miguel Valley declined in political importance. Over time it evolved into, what is today, a peaceful and relatively obscure farming and ranching region.

Of all the old San Miguel Valley settlements discussed here, only Cucurpe can be accessed by paved road. Sadly, the historic church of Cucurpe is in ruins. The once important mission settlement of Pópulo has disappeared except for scattered clumps of adobe. Fortunately, fascinating small historic churches continue to serve the inhabitants of Nacámeri, Opodepe, Los Ángeles and Horcasitas.

Nuestra Señora de la Asunción de Opodepe

The pillared main portal is similar to that of San Ignacio and some of the other border-lands missions. However, the facade and abutting fortress-like belltower are unique (Grabas).

Nacámeri (Rayón)

Baptisms were being conducted at Nacámeri from 1638, apparently by either Fr. Lorenzo de Cárdenas or Bartolomé de Castaño. In 1645, Fr. Francisco Paris established the mission site here as a *visita* of his *cabecera* in Ures. Except for brief periods Nacámeri would remain a *visita*: first of Ures, then Pópulo, and finally Opodepe.

Opodepe

Baptisms were being conducted at Opodepe from 1649. The first recorded Jesuit church was built in 1678. Opodepe initially became a *visita* of Cucurpe but by 1720 it had become a *cabecera* with Fr. Francisco Mestanza the resident missionary. Somewhere between 1764 and 1772 the church was destroyed or deteriorated so badly that it had to be replaced. A new adobe church, evidently the one there today, was built by the Franciscans in 1775. This church also deteriorated. It was extensively renovated in the 1950's.

This is a close-up view of the left side of the facade of the Opodepe church. The facing is covered with pictures within squares which are framed by stone ridges. Each frame holds a simple line sketch portraying a different subject. Subjects include geometric forms, fruit and vegetable forms, and human individuals and pairs involved in various activities. There is no obvious unifying theme for the drawings other than that they all apparently depict some present or past aspect of the life experience of the local culture (Grabas).

Los Ángeles

Los Ángeles was established as a Seri community and as a *visita* of Pópulo shortly after 1700. Although it never became important as a mission site or civilian community and was deserted in 1751 along with Pópulo, it was later repopulated. Early this century, it experienced some temporary invigoration from the establishment of a textile factory there. The factory subsequently burned down and was not rebuilt. The population declined and the community church fell into ruin. Los Ángeles still has a small population. Recently, steps have been taken to restore the church.

Nuestra Señora de Guadalupe La Reina de los Ángeles

The exact age of this church is unknown. In its present form, it was probably built around the first decade of the twentieth century. However, it may be the reconstruction of a eighteenth century Jesuit church which served the Seri. Its high walls support a vaulted ceiling. Its nave is complemented by two shallow transepts with modest but attractive altars and retablos (Walter).

Horcasitas

The cornerstone for the church of San Miguel de Horcasitas was laid in 1749, the year the presidio was established. The church, which was to be the presidio's chapel, was built the following year with captive Seri labor. It has never been a mission church. Its earliest parishioners were Spanish colonists and it has always been staffed by secular clergy.

San Miguel Arcángel de Horcasitas

This graceful eighteenth century church dominates the town plaza. Although there is no resident priest, the church is cared for by members of the Franciscan Eucharistic Sisters of San José who live in an adjacent dwelling (Walter).

San Miguel Arcángel de Horcasitas

Its well-maintained interior holds a wealth of fascinating antique objects. Recent efforts to remove whitewash from the walls of the sacristy revealed decorative drawings of an unknown age (Walter).

Cucurpe

The Franciscans arrived in Cucurpe about 1645. The Jesuits began to visit there around 1650. Fr. Gaspar Tomás was the first resident Jesuit. He arrived sometime before 1678 and built the first known church. Tomás was succeeded by Fr. Pedro Castellanos who, in turn, was succeeded by Fr. José Aguilar. Fr. Aguilar was the resident when Fr. Eusebio Kino arrived there to begin his work in the *Pimería Alta*.

Aguilar was replaced by a succession of other Jesuits and, except for one 10-year period, Cucurpe remained a *cabecera* until the Jesuit expulsion. Its last resident Jesuit was Ignacio Pfefferkorn whose *Description of the Province of Sonora* was published shortly before his death and has been reprinted over time in various languages. The mission's first Franciscan resident, Fr. Antonio de los Reyes, stayed for three years. Fr. Reyes became the first bishop of the new Diocese of Sonora established in the following decade.

Nuestra Señora de Los Dolores de Cósari

Fr. Kino arrived here in early 1687 and quickly built a chapel. About two years later, the first and only church to be there was built. A little to the north of Cósari, he established a *visita* at a Pima settlement named Doágibubig. This he named Nuestra Señora de los Remedios. An impressive church was built at Remedios at the same time the church of Cocóspera was being built. The two were said to be almost identical in appearance.

While Kino was alive this mission thrived but, after his death in 1711, the problems of epidemics and Apache attacks proved too much for the inhabitants. By 1730, Remedios had fallen into ruin. By 1732, the mission of Dolores was reported to be all but abandoned. In 1739, after a smallpox epidemic had reduced an already shrunken population, the mission was formally disestablished. The remaining populations of Dolores and Remedios were consolidated by Fr. Ignacio Keller at Cocóspera. At that point, Cocóspera became a *visita* of Fr. Keller's mission of Suamca.

Today there are no substantive ruins at Dolores or Remedios to capture the interest of the curious.

Opposite: These house ruins at the Cucurpe mission site may be those of the residence of Padre Salvador Peña, built in the 1750's
(Grabas).

Los Santos Reyes de Cucurpe

The church ruins are located on a mesa above the town. They consist of an assortment of adobe, fired brick, and hewn stone forming both finished and completed but deteriorating walls and arches from different periods. The ruins incorporate the remnants of three churches built on the same site at different times. There is little evidence of the original church. However, the adobe walls of the second church, constructed in the eighteenth century, are still intact. The walls of the third church, which was never finished, were constructed with stone slabs up to a height of four feet and, above, with adobe. Several brick arches are in place from this third effort and the combination of walls and arches define the space and dimensions that were to characterize the church's final form (Grabas).

San Miguel Arcángel de Oposura

The facade is styled with three registers, vertically united by four sets of columns and pilasters that lead to a skyline embellished with spiral and cone and ball forms. A large cross at the centerpoint of the skyline gives crowning symmetry to a balanced set of large windows and niches (Grabas).

Chapter 8
The Northeastern River Valleys

The Northeastern Valley mission churches are most directly reached by traveling from Douglas, Arizona to Agua Prieta and, from there, south along Mexican Highway #17 to Moctezuma. On the south side of Agua Prieta, make a right at the 'T' intersection and look for the left turn onto Highway #17 a short distance beyond. This is a typical two-lane rural road (one lane each way). At points it is crossed by streams which may be hazardous in rainy seasons. The Moctezuma church is in the town's central plaza. To continue on to Bacadéhuachi, take a left on the south side of town and take Route #69 to the end of the pavement at El Coyote. Route #69 is paved but is a winding, mountainside road subject to rock falls. Beyond El Coyote the road is gravel-based to an intersection with two dirt-based branches, one leading north and the other south. Take the south branch to Bacadéhuachi. This is a winding road with considerable vertical variation in places. In the best of times (that is to say in dry seasons after being re-graded), this last leg is passable to 2-wheel drive passenger vehicles. However, generally, a 4-wheel drive vehicle is recommended.

East of the Sonora River Valley, and apace with missionary activity there and in the San Miguel Valley, Jesuits were advancing among the Ópata people in the remote valleys of the upper Moctezuma and Bavispe Rivers. In 1644, Frs. Marcos del Río and Egidio Montefrío became active in the Moctezuma River Valley. As previously mentioned, Río and Montefrío were Belgians who had taken Spanish-sounding names.

Montefrío built churches at Oposura (today Moctezuma) and Cumpas. Two years later, Río established a mission at Huásabas on the lower Bavispe River. Meanwhile, another Jesuit, Cristóbol García established a mission site to the east of Huásabas, at Bacadéhuachi.

Oposura, close to mining operations at San Juan Bautista, was selected by Governor Perea to be Sonora's first capital. This is the period in which Perea introduced Franciscans into Sonora, and the Franciscan friar Juan Suarez became especially active in the area although the Franciscans built no missions.

Miners had preceded missionaries into this region. The mission community and the mining towns were two very different environments, As the two grew side-by-side, assimilation of the Indian population was more irregular than in parts of the borderlands where the missionaries arrived first. Indians who worked in the mines were more directly exposed to Spanish colonial society than those in mission farm and cattle communities. They were also more exposed to economic exploitation.

By 1651, and largely through the efforts of Río and Montefrío, a number of mission churches had been established on the Bavispe River. Substantial churches were built in the communities of Bavispe, Huásabas and Bacerac. By the 1670's, mission stations were in place along the entire lengths of the Moctezuma and Bavispe River valleys. However, the colonial development of this rugged, mountainous region progressed very slowly.

The effects of Apache hostility were especially severe as the northeastern river valleys were directly along the axis of Apache movement into Sonora. Yaqui bands also raided this area. As was the case in the northern Sonora River Valley, warfare with marauding Indians exacted a heavy toll on the Ópata population and, along with epidemics of infectious diseases, caused a significant population decline over time. The Spanish were never able to truly control or pacify the Apache during the colonial period. Difficult terrain and the relative remoteness of

San Luis Gonzaga de Bacadéhuachi

The unusual concave face of this eighteenth century Jesuit church is accentuated by three registers, each of highly detailed and distinctive design, separated by decorative cornices and capped with two matching belltowers (Above and Opposite by Walter).

this region made the Upper Moctezuma and Bavispe valleys all the more difficult to protect.

In 1887, an unusually strong earthquake struck the Arizona-Sonora borderlands with particularly serious consequences for communities in the Sierra Madre Occidental. Old churches and church ruins were devastated. The imposing old adobe church at Bavispe was destroyed. The church at Bacadéhuachi was badly damaged.

Two beautiful churches of the missionary period have survived in the northeastern river valleys of Sonora, one at Oposura on the Moctezuma River and the other at Bacadéhuachi near the Bavispe River. Moctezuma has been the larger and more important of the two towns in the region over time. Its mission was generally the more important of the two during the Jesuit period.

San Luis Gonzaga de Bacadéhuachi

Moctezuma (Oposura)

The mission station at Oposura was established in the 1640's as a *visita* of Cumpas. In 1653, with the arrival of Fr. Juan Uter as resident, Oposura became a *cabecera*. After Montefrío left Cumpas, Cumpas became a *visita* of Oposura. In 1687, Kino met the Jesuit Visitor, Padre Manuel González, and Fr. José de Aguilar, the resident missionary of Cucurpe at Oposura. Prior to Kino's arrival, González and Aguilar had already determined the general course of action Kino should follow. From Oposura, they led Kino to Cucurpe. It was from Cucurpe that Kino was to make his first move north to Cósari on the San Miguel River.

The church at Moctezuma has been rebuilt a number of times. By 1678, through the efforts of resident missionary Fr. Juan Martínez, it had reputedly become one of the most beautiful churches in the Province. Martínez was succeeded by Manuel González. After González died in 1702, Fr. Daniel Janusque, formerly of Tubutama, became resident missionary until 1724.

Fr. Janusque began the last major rebuilding of the church, employing artisans whom he brought to Oposura at great expense. Construction continued under another missionary named Manuel González, Janusque's replacement. It was finished in 1738, under the residency of Fr. Buenaventura Gutiérrez. Since then, the church has undergone additional remodeling, to include significant changes to the facade. It is a large beautiful church with a vaulted ceiling and an octagonal chapel. It holds the distinction of being the only colonial building on the Moctezuma River that remains substantially intact.

Bacadéhuachi

It appears that the first mission was established here by Fr. Cristóbol García in 1645 at the site of a small Ópata settlement. It is uncertain when the first church was built at Bacadéhuachi. However, it is known that either a mission station or *cabecera* was in existence in 1662 under the charge of the Jesuit Juan Betancur. Betancur's successor, Fr. Luis Davila, maintained his *cabercera* at nearby Nácori. In 1709, Fr. Nicolás del Oro arrived to take charge of mission activities in the area and established his *cabecera* at Bacadéhuachi. Oro is credited with building the existing church which was embellished over time by his successors. Fr. Jesus Manuel Aguirre was the resident at the time of the Jesuit expulsion.

The church of San Luis Gonzaga de Bacadéhuachi is the most remote and most remarkably unique of the Sonoran frontier mission churches. It features a highly decorative concave facade, a diversity of domes and towers, a complex interior floor plan, and rich furnishings.

Interior view of the nave of San Miguel Arcángel de Oposura (Walter).

Interior view of the nave of San Luis Gonzaga de Bacadéhuachi (Walter).

Main dome of Nuestro Padre San Ignacio de Cabórica (Jaime).

Chapter 9
Magdalena River Valley
C

The Magdalena Valley mission sites are located along Mexican Federal Highway #15. This highway is most easily reached from Arizona at Nogales. The historic church at Ímuris is reached by turning right off of Highway #15 at the Padre Kino statue in that town, and following the main town street to the central plaza. The mission site at Cocóspera is reached by taking Mexican Federal Highway #2 east from Ímuris for about 26 miles. A sign to a private farm settlement named Cocóspera is along the south side of the road, just west of the mission site. The church ruins are just barely visible a short distance beyond, on the highground north of Highway #2. A dirt road off of Highway #2 directly accesses the mission ruins. The mission site at San Ignacio is reached by taking the north exit to Magdalena from Highway #15. Prior to Magdalena a road sign identifies the .right-hand turn onto the local road to San Ignacio. The historic church and site of Kino's remains in Magdalena are located in that town's central plaza, located on the town's southwest side. Look for signs and the church steeple from along the town's main "through" street.

Eusebio Kino's jump from the San Miguel Valley into the Magdalena Valley would precipitate two other rapid moves he would make: one into the Altar Valley to the west and the other into the Santa Cruz Valley to the north, toward Tucson. As had been the strategy of other Jesuits before him, Kino sought existing population centers for the sites of his missions. Pima Indians populated all three of these river drainage systems.

He established his first two sites in the Magdalena Valley in 1687 at San Ignacio and Ímuris. By 1689 he had established another mission station upriver, on a branch of the Magdalena, at Cocóspera. In 1690 he established a *visita* at Magdalena. These stations were initially *visitas*, administered from his headquarters at Dolores. After San Ignacio become a *cabecera*, Magdalena and Ímuris fell under its jurisdiction.

Religious services were also provided to other settlements on a less regular basis. An old church, possibly from the missionary period, is located at the outskirts of modern-day Santa Ana in what is known as Santa Ana Vieja.

San Ignacio

The *visita* of San Ignacio was established at the Pima *ranchería* of Cabórica. It was named after the founder of the Jesuit order, Saint Ignatius of Loyola. Its first resident missionary, assigned in 1690, was Fr. Luis Maria Pineli. With the arrival Augustín Campos, in 1693, a church was built.

Circular mesquite stairway to the roof of the church of San Ignacio. This
staircase design, known as "caracol" (Spanish for "snail") is duplicated in
the stone staircase to the bell platform at the Cucurpe mission church
ruins. The remains of a wooden caracol staircase are also found in the
church ruins of Cocóspera (Grabas).

Detail of the old carved wooden door of the main portal of the church of San Ignacio. This door is made of mesquite planks (Grabas).

Father Campos became a critical Jesuit link of continuity in Kino's area. He was to enjoy a 43-year period of residency at San Ignacio. His mission was the only one established by Kino to retain a resident missionary after Kino's death. Campos, in an effort to fill Kino's shoes, himself became a tireless traveler, maintaining contact with the mission sites to the north that had reverted to the status of *visitas*. His travels extended even further north than those of Kino, at one point reaching into Arizona's White Mountains. He also visited the Yuma Indians on the Colorado River. In the process of traveling, he became a "saddle" friend of Juan Bautista de Anza (the Elder). Campos remained active until 1736.

San Ignacio remained the center of Kino's old rectorate until the expulsion of the Jesuits in 1767. Fray Diego Martin García became the first Franciscan to be

Nuestro Padre San Ignacio de Cabórica

Franciscan reconstruction of this church largely preserved its earlier Jesuit character. Buttresses support massive walls. Decoration on the facade is limited to geometric forms on the skyline and ornamentation around the portal and large round overhead window. The external appearance is further characterized by two domes and a two-tiered belltower (Grabas).

assigned in 1768. Afterwards, it stayed important for awhile although its role was ultimately eclipsed by the missions at Caborca, Tubutama, and San Xavier del Bac. In 1827, with the Mexican law banishing the Spanish-born from the country, San Ignacio became the seat of Fr. José Pérez Llera, one of the only two missionaries left in Sonora. Llera administered all the missions of the Altar Valley from San Ignacio.

By this point, the mission system was in decline. When Kino's old territory was ultimately consolidated into the Diocese of Sonora, the operational significance of San Ignacio dropped further. The mission church became a village temple of worship and, in effect, a *visita* of the Magdalena parish.

Rooftop view of the domed stairway of San Ignacio, as seen from the belltower (Grabas).

Some small communities in the Magdalena Valley hold post- missionary period churches that are, nonetheless, old and worth a visit while enroute to others of relatively greater historical importance. Two such churches are located in Ímuris (below) and Santa Ana Vieja (above) (Grabas).

Ímuris

Ímuris was first visited by Kino and Fr. Jose Aguilar in March 1687, within days of Kino's initial visit to Cósari and Cabórica. Fr. Pedro Sandoval was briefly assigned there in 1691 and a chapel was built. The mission station was sacked in 1695 and the chapel destroyed. Shortly afterwards a spacious church was built that served until it was heavily damaged in 1776.

The mission station at Ímuris never became as important as the stations at San Ignacio and Magdalena. The existing church, thought to be the fifth, is a reconstruction of a church built in 1851. Its greatest distinction is being the repository of a large old wooden crucifix with a carved Christ, painted black until recently. The date of this image's carving is unknown, as is the identity of the artist. However, it has been identified as the most notable of the religious relics taken from Tucson by Mexican soldiers in 1856 after the Gadsden Purchase. This piece of art, called the "Cristo Negro" is loosely modeled after the Black Christ of Esquipulas carved by Quirio Cataño in the late 1500's. The Ímuris crucifix was recently repainted polychrome.

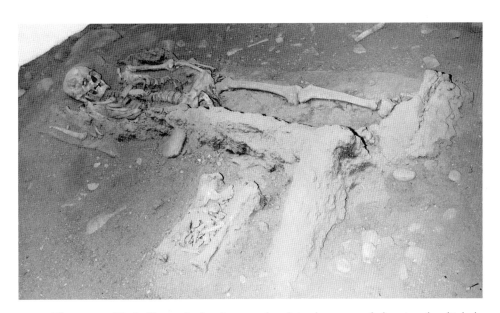

The remains of Padre Kino as displayed in a windowed circular crypt at the location where his body was discovered by a team of scientists in 1966 (Grabas).

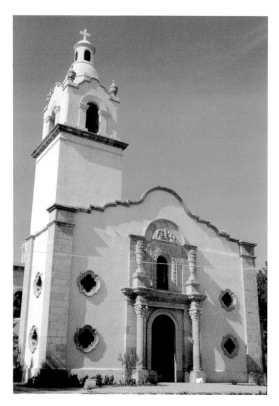

Above: A view of the church of Santa Maria Magdalena de Buquivaba. This church was constructed on a site about 100 yards from the original mission church (Walter).
Below: An interior view of Santa Maria de Magdalena looking toward the main altar (Jaime).

Nuestra Señora del Pilar y Santiago de Cocóspera

The Franciscan church was built using the foundation and walls of the earlier Jesuit church. The Jesuit walls of sun-dried adobe block were sandwiched between burnt brick walls added by the Franciscans. The brick exterior walls were then surfaced with stucco. The church had two belltowers and a vaulted roof. After the mission was abandoned, the church declined into a ruined state from the combined effects of vandals, treasure and souvenir seekers, and the weather. Its presence, however, still dominates the old river terrace on which it sits (Grabas).

Magdalena

While Magdalena was not as important as San Ignacio as a mission station, it became, over time, more important than the latter as a colonial settlement. The original mission church, completed by Fr. Campos in 1711, is gone. Kino died after becoming ill during the dedication mass for a chapel built adjacent to it. Kino was buried in the chapel but, after the church and chapel were destroyed, the burial site was forgotten. The site was rediscovered in 1966 and became the inspiration for a beautiful new plaza.

The existing church was built by the Franciscan Fr. José Pérez Llera between 1803 and 1832 and was significantly remodeled in the 1950's.

The new plaza, designed by Francisco Artigas, encompasses 15 acres and is enclosed on all sides by buildings with portaled walkways. A large fountain provides the centerpiece. Kino's grave site is enclosed and preserved in a memorial at one end of the plaza, with the current church at the opposite end.

Cocóspera

The Pima village of Cocóspera was located on a branch of the Magdalena River, about 37 miles northeast of the settlement of Magdalena. Kino apparently first visited the village in 1689. He established his mission site on the nearby highground overlooking the river valley. By 1691 there was a temporary temple of worship in place. Between 1691 and 1693, three Jesuits, in turn, operated from Cocóspera for short periods of time. In 1697, Father Pedro Ruiz de Contreras was assigned as resident priest. He found a well-furnished mission on the site and the beginnings of a church which he finished. In 1698, shortly after its completion, the mission was attacked and laid to ruins by a group of Apaches, Sumas, and Jocomes.

Mission functions were quickly restored and a temporary church was in operation by 1700. Construction of a larger, more permanent church was undertaken in 1702. It was built and dedicated concurrently with the mission church at Remedios in 1704. The effort was supervised in considerable measure by Kino himself.

The population around the mission declined rapidly after Kino's death and Cocóspera became a *visita* of Suamca. In 1746, the mission was again attacked by hostile Indians and substantially destroyed. The church was repaired and continued to serve as a *visita* of Suamca until the Jesuit expulsion. For awhile, Fr. Francisco Hlawa was assigned as the resident.

In 1768, resources of Suamca were shifted to Cocóspera, and it again gained a resident missionary, the Franciscan Fr. Francisco Roche. By this point, the Cocóspera church had seriously deteriorated and required extensive reconstruction. Credit for the work subsequently accomplished is given to the Franciscan

Friar Juan Antonio de Santiestevan who, it was said, transformed the severely damaged Jesuit adobe structure into an elegant church of Neo-classic design. This structure was badly damaged by another Apache attack in 1776 and another construction (or reconstruction) took place. A succession of missionaries resided at Cocóspera until 1836, the last one being Rafael Díaz. It was finally abandoned about 1845 because of continued Apache attacks.

Nuestra Señora del Pilar y Santiago de Cocóspera

View of the nave looking toward the sanctuary and main retablo. The remains of highly decorative plaster motifs can still be seen. The design of a vase filled with a spray of pomegranates is located above each of two large niches of the retablo. The design on the left is intact. The one on the right appears to have been vandalized by booty hunters (Grabas).

View of the nave of the church from the sanctuary (Grabas).

This door in the collapsing arcade wall of the Caborca mission in the Altar Valley seems to lead into nowhere. It probably once led to the mission's interior garden (Richards).

Chapter 10
Altar River Valley
℮

The Altar Valley mission churches are best reached by traveling Mexican Federal Highway #15 to the intersection with Federal Highway #2 at Santa Ana. Travel west on Highway #2 to Altar. To reach the mission churches of Oquitoa and Tubutama, turn right off of Highway #2 at the west edge of Altar and travel north on Highway #43. Highway #43 is a poorly marked rural road (two lanes, one lane each way). The turn-off is at a three-corner intersection just west of a modern municipal government building on the south side of Highway #2. To reach the mission churches of Pitiquito and Caborca, continue west on Highway #2 past Altar, to Caborca. Pitiquito is on the south side of the highway enroute. It has a well-marked access road. Further west, Highway #2 skirts the north side of Caborca. The old Kino mission church is in a residential area on the south side of town on a north-south street that intersects with the highway. The street's name is Calzada 6 de Abril.

Leaving his new followers in the San Miguel and Magdalena Valleys with the tasks of mission construction and consolidation, Eusebio Kino moved on to his next target area for evangelization, the Altar Valley. His initial focus was the upper Altar where, by the end of 1689, he had made contact with about 1200 Indians in *rancherías* around Tubutama and northward. Two years later he turned to the south, toward what is, today, Caborca.

Kino's rapid success in the Altar, as well as previously in the San Miguel and Magdalena Valleys, can, in significant measure, be attributed to the effective support rendered him by his Indian guides. Most notable among them was a Piman from his first mission site at Cósari named Coxi. By the time Kino entered the Altar Valley, Coxi's service had earned the Indian the Spanish title of captain-general of all the Pima.

The use of missionized natives from one area to promote the spread of the mission system to other areas, however, could be volatile. This practice contributed to the first of the two major Pima uprisings, both of which would spring from the Altar Valley. Kino would be available to mend the damage from the first uprising. He would not be in the case of the second.

After Kino's death in 1711, other Jesuits carried on his work in the Altar Valley. But the Altar and the Santa Cruz Valleys were at the extreme ends of a system with attenuated resources. The Franciscans followed the Jesuits and tried to maintain the vitality produced by earlier efforts. However, the relative success of both orders was limited by circumstances beyond the control of even the most dedicated individuals. The effective physical reach of the mission system had reached its geographic limits in view of the lack of civil government support for

San Pedro y San Pablo de Tubutama

This church is the most impressive of the missionary-era churches in the Altar Valley. Its beautiful facade and belltower dominate Tubutama's central plaza. The town and church are reached by fording the Altar River. The church's design is unusual in that, while the facade and main entrance face the plaza, they are along a side of the church rather than at the end opening into the nave, opposite the sanctuary (Grabas).

its continued role in the life of the region.

The most remote of the mission stations established in the Altar region by Kino, at Sonóyta, survived only till the violent death of its first resident missionary, Fr. Enrique Ruhen, in 1751. Two other missions, at Sáric and Átil, were continued into the Franciscan period but fell prey to the Apaches in the early nineteenth century. Today, only deteriorated wall sections mark the locations of the latter two mission church sites. Nothing remains of the mission church at Sonóyta.

Several churches were built by the Franciscans in the Altar that have survived till today. The Jesuits had built their churches with sun-dried adobe that needed constant maintenance. The Franciscans rebuilt these churches using fired brick and lime mortar. Following is a discussion of those that remain.

Tubutama

Kino established a *visita* here in 1690. The following year, the Guatemalan born Fr. Antonio Arías arrived and began the first of several constructions and reconstructions the mission would experience. Tubutama quickly became an important *cabecera*. Over time, it would have up to six *visitas* in and near the upper Altar River Valley.

In 1693, Padre Daniel Januske, a Czech Jesuit, replaced Arías. Januske was to have a varied and challenging career in frontier Sonora that would include assignments to other missions and service as visitor. Tubutama was his initiation. In 1695, events there sparked the first of the two general Pima uprisings. Antagonisms generated by an Ópata overseer caused the local Pimas to rebel, kill the overseer and destroy the mission. Padre Januske escaped and was reassigned elsewhere. Kino did not assign another missionary to residence at Tubutama until 1701. Meanwhile, the repentant Indians rebuilt their church.

In 1701, Fr. Ignacio Iturmendi became resident missionary, but he died after barely one year. In 1703, Kino assigned the Sardinian Gerónimo Minutuli to Tubutama. He, together with Kino, built a bigger, finer church than the one reconstructed by the Indians. Minutuli was succeeded by Fr. Luis Marciano and in 1727, Marciano, in turn, was succeeded by Luis Gallardi who served there until his death in 1736. During these transitions, Tubutama was sometimes without a resident Jesuit for considerable periods and reverted to *visita* status. Somewhere between Marciano's and Gallardi's tenures, something, now unknown, happened to the church that Kino and Minituli built and Gallardi built a new one.

The Bavarian Jacobo Sedelmayr became Tubutama's resident missionary in the 1740's. Sedelmayr revitalized the mission's role through a variety of initiatives, to include the building of still another church. Sedelmayr was often away from Tubutama, traveling extensively, including as far north as what is, today, central Arizona along the Gila and Colorado Rivers. His reports on these trips stimulated increased interest in the land link between New Spain and California.

In 1751, during Sedelmayr's tenure, Tubutama was again at the center of Pima revolt. This time, the revolt was not precipitated by mission events. Tubutama was simply close to the whereabouts of the revolt's main conspirators. Sedelmayr was besieged in the mission church. The church was destroyed and Sedelmayr was wounded. The revolt was short and the mission was rebuilt. Sedelmayr, however, was reassigned from Tubutama. And, while he continued to serve in Sonora until the Jesuit expulsion, it appears he never fully regained the physical vitality that had so distinguished his activity prior to the revolt.

It was two years after the revolt before another missionary, Fr. Luis Vivas, was assigned to Tubutama. And, it wasn't until 1764 that a new church was completed. Fr. Vivas remained at Tubutama until the Jesuit expulsion. At times, he not

Left and Opposite:
The Tubutama church features a beautiful dome on a high octagonal drum, a highly decorative barrel vaulted ceiling, and two transepts. The above view is looking up into the dome and captures the upper portion of the north transept and its retablo (Grabas). This transept features symbols of the Resurrection and is the more striking of the two. Its ambience is enhanced by natural light that penetrates the transept. The theme of the south transept is complementary. The latter transept features symbols of the Crucifixion and was designed to remain in relative darkness. The opposite view is from the main altar toward the choir loft (Walter).

only had to provide for his own *visitas* but for those of other nearby *cabeceras* left without missionaries.

In 1768, the Mexican-born Fr. Mariano Buena, the first head of the Franciscan missions in the *Pimería Alta*, established himself at Tubutama. That same year, Fr. Buena moved his headquarters to Caborca and stationed Fr. Joseph del Río at Tubutama. Another new church was built; the one that is seen today. The construction of this church is credited primarily to Fray Antonio Barbastro, who was stationed here from 1776 to 1783. Tubutama was, for a time, to remain an important mission center for the Franciscans. It was served by a succession of Franciscans into the early nineteenth century, including Fr. Narciso Gutiérrez, the builder of the mission church one now sees at Tumacácori.

San Antonio Paduano de Oquitoa

This picturesque little church with its twin-arched, wall-type belfry sits on a hilltop on the edge of the small community of Oquitoa. It is surrounded on one side and at the rear by a colorful assortment of grave markers and tombs. Its unusual facade features a double tier of pilasters framed by an arching line that terminates in a cusp. The facade incorporates five statuary niches which are empty. The portal is decorated with scalloped shaped curves much like that of the church of Tubutama. The use of scallop shell decoration over doors and windows became a prominent feature of Spanish architecture beginning in the late Gothic Period because of its association with the cult of Santiago (St. James) and his role as patron of Spain (Grabas).

Opposite: The cemetery surrounding the church of San Antonio Paduano de Oquitoa (Grabas).

Oquitoa

Oquitoa lies about 21 miles south of Tubutama. It was established as a Jesuit *visita* in 1690 and later became a station of the Tubutama mission. It remained a *visita* for the Franciscans until near the end of the eighteenth century, when it became a *cabecera* for about the last 30 years of Franciscan presence in the Altar Valley. The first resident Franciscan was Fr. Francisco Moyano, who transferred his *cabecera* there from Átil.

A church was built by the Jesuits somewhere around 1730. It is probable that the existing church is the original structure, repaired and enhanced by the Franciscans. It has been restored a number of times, most recently in 1980, each time with the goal of retaining its early Jesuit character.

La Purisima Concepción de Nuestra Señora de Caborca

Above: The mission church, formerly at the center of community activity, sits in what has become a quiet residential neighborhood of a large, modern agricultural city. The basic architectural design is the same as that of the church of San Xavier del Bac. An arch in the plaza in front of the church is from the cemetery gateway of the early Jesuit church at Batuc, on the Moctezuma River. Batuc was intentionally submerged by the Mexican government to create a dam (Grabas).

Opposite: The Caborca church is located on the banks of the Asunción River, just to the southwest of the Altar River Valley. It has suffered heavily from floods and other destructive forces over time. While it has been partially restored, it no longer serves as a temple of worship.

Caborca

Caborca is located on the Concepción River, to the west of but near the Altar. Kino first arrived in the Caborca vicinity in 1693. The following year, Padre Francisco Xavier Saeta, a Sicilian, was assigned as resident there and a church was built. During the Pima Revolt of 1695, Saeta was killed and the church destroyed. Kino began building a new church in 1702, but it is not clear when it was finished or what happened to it afterwards. While Kino made an effort to maintain Caborca as a *cabecera*, missionaries assigned there rarely remained long and the mission center was often without a resident Jesuit. At times it was serviced as a *visita* of Tubutama.

Between 1702 and 1727, Caborca was served by a succession of Jesuits to include Luis Velarde, Luis Gallardi, and Luis Marciano, all of whom also served for longer periods at other Kino missions. It appears that Marciano was the last resident until Fr. José Torres Perea arrived in 1743. By that time, Kino's second church at Caborca had disappeared. Torres began a third church but he died in 1747. The church was probably completed in 1750, three Jesuits later, by Fr. Tómas Tello.

In 1751, the second of the Pima revolts dealt a crushing blow to the Caborca mission. Tello was murdered and the church was badly damaged. Other Jesuits

followed, but only one, the Bavarian Fr. Antonio Benz, was to stay any appreciable time before the Jesuit expulsion. Meanwhile the church was repaired and improved well enough to serve the mission until the coming of the Franciscans.

Fray Juan Díaz was the first of the Franciscan missionaries at Caborca, arriving in 1768. However, it was not until 35 years later that another Franciscan, Fray Andrés Sanchez, undertook the building of the present church. It was completed in 1809, just before the outbreak of the Mexican Wars of Independence. This church was the last of the significant building efforts by the Franciscans in the *Pimería Alta* to reach completion. Its principal builder was Ignacio Gaona, the same mason/architect generally credited for the construction of the existing church at Mission San Xavier del Bac. In 1827, with the passing of the Mexican law banning all those born in Spain from Mexico, Franciscan resources dried-up and Caborca once again reverted to a *visita*.

One of the most interesting events in the church's history occurred after the missionary period. In 1857, a North American adventurer, Henry Crabb, and his accomplices were executed on the church's steps by a firing squad after Crabb and his private army had invaded Sonora and tried taking control of the region by force.

San Diego de Pitiquito

The town of Pitiquito lies nears the junction of the Asunción, Magdalena and Altar Rivers. The church is on a small rise, near the center of town. It is an impressive eighteenth century structure with little exterior ornamentation. The two-tiered belltower is a replacement for an earlier wall-type double belfry similar to the one at Oquitoa (Grabas).

View of the Pitiquito church from the southwest showing the dome of an attached room, probably part of the destroyed convento, in the foreground and the main church dome to the rear (Jaime).

Pitiquito

This mission station was established at a *ranchería* site named Pitiquin sometime prior to 1695 as a visita of Caborca. A church was constructed by Kino around 1706 but it disappeared by 1730. A ramada was used for religious purposes until a second church was built near the end of the Jesuit period. This church, taken over by Fr. Juan Díaz as the first Franciscan at Caborca, was described by him as a partially destroyed and relatively empty adobe structure with a straw and dirt roof.

The present church is built of stone and burnt brick and presents a very austere appearance. It was built by the Franciscans beginning in 1778. The interior is divided into bays by pilasters (wall columns) which support a barrel vaulted roof and dome. The overall effect is that of solidity and massiveness.

The Pitiquito church is perhaps best known for its catechetical artwork on its interior walls. This work was discovered under layers of whitewash when the walls were scrubbed clean using modern commercial detergents in 1967. The history of these large religious murals is unknown, having been created earlier than the institutional memory of the parish, presumably in the colonial period. Several of the drawings are complete and quite distinct (Grabas).

The mortuary chapel and graveyard of the Tumacácori mission church (Grabas).

Chapter 11
Santa Cruz River Valley
$\mathcal{C}^{m}$

The Santa Cruz Valley mission sites are located along U.S. Interstate Highway #19, between Tucson and Nogales, Arizona. Highway signs identify exits to San Xavier and Tumacácori. The ruins of Guévavi and Calabasas are south of Tumacácori and are managed by the National Park Service office at Tumacácori National Historical Park. Access to these ruins is by special permission and guided tour only.

Eusebio Kino began to extend his mission district into modern-day Arizona in 1691, the year after his early initiatives in the Altar Valley. In his first trip he traveled north along the Santa Cruz River as far as Tumacácori. The following year he traveled along the Santa Cruz and San Pedro River basins, visiting Pima settlements along both these valleys to include the settlement of Bac near modern-day Tucson.

In the ensuing years Kino expanded his explorations north to the Gila River and west to the Colorado. In the course of that period, he made repeat visits to sites along the Santa Cruz that he began to prepare as mission stations. However, it was not until the turn of the century that he actually established missions in modern-day Arizona. In 1701, he assigned missionaries to Guévavi and Bac and established a *visita* at Tumacácori.

Other mission stations were also established about the same time near the headwaters of the Santa Cruz at Suamca, San Lázaro and San Luis Bacoancos. However, it was not until 1732 that these last stations, which were south of the modern U.S.-Mexico boundary, gained much attention. In that year, Fr. Ignacio Keller arrived at Suamca and established a *cabecera* there. Suamca was to remain important until the Jesuit expulsion in 1767.

Kino lacked the resources to establish missions along the San Pedro and Gila Rivers, although there was Indian interest to support them. Some humble *visitas* were established along the lower Gila and Colorado Rivers but all of their traces have long since disappeared. It proved difficult enough for the Jesuits to maintain the stations along the Santa Cruz. All of these sites went for protracted periods without resident missionaries.

Suamca and Guévavi were abandoned shortly after the expulsion of the Jesuits due to an inability to protect them from Apache attacks. Tumacácori suffered a similar fate in 1848. While the settlement of Suamca would be later reestablished as the site of a presidio, no physical trace of its earlier important missionary role survived.

View of the church ruins of San José de Tumacácori from a portal of the Tumacácori National Historical Park Museum (Walter).

The mission sites of San Xavier and Tumacácori ultimately benefited by the Gadsden Purchase of 1853, which incorporated them into U.S. territory. Before the end of the century, the U.S. Army had pacified the Apaches. In the twentieth century considerable effort has been invested in preserving the historic churches at these locations. Lesser attention has been paid to Guévavi and Calabasas which are now managed by the U.S. Park Service. Here, there are only badly deteriorated ruins.

Los Santos Ángeles de Guévavi

Kino selected this site on the east bank of the Santa Cruz because of its proximity to Pima *rancherías* in the area. It holds the distinction of being Arizona's first Jesuit mission. Fr. Juan de San Martín was assigned as resident missionary in 1701. However, he remained less than half a year and the mission was soon abandoned. It regained the status of *visita* but did not have another resident missionary until the arrival of Fr. Juan Bautista Grashoffer in 1732. Grashoffer and his successor, Felipe Ségesser, were only there for a total of two years. Subsequently, and until 1737, Guévavi was administered by the missionaries of San Xavier and Suamca.

Guévavi enjoyed its first stable period as a *cabecera* in the period 1737-1741, when Frs. Alexandro Rapicani and José Torres Perea served there successively.

The next resident missionary of any duration was Fr. José Garrucho who served from 1745 till November 1751 when the mission was substantially destroyed in the Pima Rebellion.

Guévavi was rebuilt and reestablished as a Jesuit *cabecera* in 1753. It retained its *cabecera* status until after the Jesuit expulsion. For a while, it served visitas at Tumacácori, Calabasas, and Sonoitac. The Franciscans transferred *cabecera* functions from there to Tumacácori in 1771. Among its resident missionaries for a time was Ignacio Pfefferkorn. Its last Jesuit was Fr. Custodio Xímeno. Xímeno was not replaced until a year after the Jesuit expulsion. His successor, the Franciscan Fray Juan Chrisóstomo Gil de Bernave stayed three years until he was carried from the mission, a sick man. Guévavi again became a *visita*. By 1775, it was totally abandoned, a victim of incessant Apache attacks.

San José de Tumacácori

This mission station was established at the Indian village of Tumacácori in 1701. It remained a visita through most of the Jesuit period. The initial mission complex was built in 1732 by the Guévavi resident missionary, Fr. Grashoffer. The mission station began to increase in importance after 1751, when a Spanish presidio was established nearby at Tubac. For a while after the Franciscans arrived, Tubac served as a *cabecera*. Its fortunes began to wane in 1776 when the Spanish Crown transferred its military garrison from Tubac to Tucson.

The current mission complex was built under Franciscan direction in 1773 and reconstructed at various times. About 1800, its resident missionary Fray Narciso Gutiérrez began to build the extant church which, although now in ruins, has been somewhat restored. This church was never properly completed. Its construction was delayed by the Mexican Wars of Independence and was virtually stopped by the Mexican decree which expelled Spanish-born priests from its territory. With the intent of making it serviceable, the church plan was radically simplified and a wood and mud flat roof was constructed in lieu of the planned vaulted brick roof.

By 1848, a combination of Apache attacks and bad weather forced the last residents away and Tumacácori was abandoned. The restoration of Tumacácori took place beginning in 1937 with the establishment there of a public visitor center. Tumacácori has since become a National Park.

San Xavier del Bac

Kino began to prepare Bac for a mission years before one was actually established there. He drove cattle, horses, sheep, and goats to Bac in 1697. By November of that year, the Indians had already built a substantial house for the missionary he had promised them. The foundations for the first church were laid

Santa Cruz Valley Ruins

Above: These are the only visible remains of Arizona's first Jesuit mission headquarters, Los Santos Ángeles de Guévavi (Grabas). The ground surrounding the standing wall segments largely consists of decomposed building material from the church and conceals about four feet of wall height and the church floor.

Below: This view is of the church ruins at Calabasas. The Calabasas ruins are better protected than those of Guévavi and somewhat more intact (Walter).

in 1700. The first resident missionary, Fr. Francisco Gonsalvo, was assigned in 1701. The following year, Gonsalvo contracted pneumonia and died. San Xavier became a *visita* of San Ignacio.

Despite the high priority that Kino had attached to San Xavier, the mission was difficult to sustain. It was at the very limit of the Jesuit reach. Until 1756 it was mostly served as a visita by missionaries based at San Ignacio and Suamca. Its first resident missionary of stable service was Fr. Alonso Espinosa who arrived there in 1756. Espinosa stayed at San Xavier till shortly prior to the Jesuit expulsion. He was replaced for a brief period by Fr. José Neve, who became the last Jesuit there.

Kino's original church was never finished. According to some sources, a church was in place in 1751 but destroyed in the Pima Revolt of that year. It may have been little more than a ramada. Something more elaborate in the way of a church structure was built by Fr. Alonso Espinosa in the period 1756-1763. Although Espinosa's church initially served the Franciscans, they constructed the more permanent existing church over the period 1777-1783.

The first Franciscan at San Xavier was Fr. Francisco Gárces. He also inherited a *visita* which had been established nearby to the northeast, San Augustín de Tucson. Gárces became an accomplished explorer, much in the style of the earlier Jesuits Kino, Sedelmayr, and Keller. Gárces accompanied the Tubac commander Juan Bautista de Anza on several trips and, in 1774 and 1775, accompanied him on trips to California which resulted in the Spanish settlement of the San Francisco Bay area. In 1779, Gárces was reassigned to mission duty near Yuma and was replaced by Fr. Joaquin Antonio Velarde, who had been at Tumacácori. Shortly afterwards, Gárces was killed in an Indian uprising near what is today Yuma, Arizona.

Fr. Velarde was replaced by Fr. Juan Bautista Velderrain somewhere around 1781. Velderrain was, in turn, replaced by Fr. Juan Baustista Llorenz. Velderrain and Llorenz were the Franciscans responsible for the building of the existing church of San Xavier del Bac. Its right belltower, however, was never finished because of a lack of funds to complete the job. Llorenz stayed at Bac until about 1814 and was then followed by others. The last Franciscan missionary there was Fr. Antonio González who left in 1836.

When the mission at Bac became secularized, it was made part of the Magdalena, Sonora parish. After the Gadsden Purchase, it was placed under the Santa Fe Diocese and was apparently served, from time to time, by priests at Tucson. Its lands were incorporated into the Pápago Indian reservation. In 1873 a school for the Pápagos was opened at the mission site and run by the Sisters of St. Joseph of Carondelet. In 1913, the mission was placed under the direction of Franciscans belonging to the Province of Santa Barbara, headquartered in California. While it is still staffed by the Franciscans it is owned by the Diocese of Tucson.

San Xavier del Bac

This church near Tucson, Arizona is the most elaborate and popular of the mission-era churches in the region (Above by Walter, below by Grabas).

San Xavier del Bac

Opposite: This view is of a colorfully painted wall section of the interior of San Xavier. The overall richness of the ambience is greatly enhanced by the many artfully constructed and painted statues which occupy wall niches inside the church (Walter).

Chapter 12
Conclusion
C

With its 1834 decree secularizing all missions on Mexican soil, the young Mexican Republic dealt the death blow to the mission system established by the religious orders. Yet, the process had been long underway, and the stage had already been set for this conclusion in actions taken by the Spanish Crown before Mexican independence.

Royal control of church affairs in the Americas had been ceded to the Spanish monarchy by Pope Julius II at the very outset of the Spanish Conquest. This was done with the understanding that the Crown would support the spread of Catholicism through its colonial framework. The monarchy would have preferred to work through a bureaucracy completely manned by church figures who were of Spanish blood and sympathetic to the worldly goals of Spain. However, the inventory of secular clergy who met those criteria was inadequate to serve the Crown's needs.

Through the first half the 18th century, the pacification of the native inhabitants of the frontier was a high priority of colonial government. In view of meager resources to apply to this objective and under difficult environmental circumstances, the resources represented by the international Catholic orders were too valuable to overlook. The missionary orders were organizationally and philosophically ideally suited for the task. Civil leadership was quick to see the practical value of the orders in disposing the independent-minded native peoples toward colonization and acculturation. Still, the mission system was always viewed as a transitional device.

As long as the missionaries were willing to promote among the Indians the idea of membership in Spanish colonial society at the bottom level, they served the broader aims of the colonial hierarchy. When, however, the missionaries balked at the outright economic exploitation of their new charges or created insulated communities that competed with the aims of colonization, they became an impediment to the Spanish view of progress. And, as colonial government gained confidence in its ability to control its frontier territories without the contributions of the orders, the missionary system as a social institution of colonial society, came under attack. First, the Jesuits were targeted for expulsion. And then the powers of the remaining missionary orders were progressively

Opposite: This view of the dome of the new parish church in Baviácora is from the arch of a collapsed transept of the early Jesuit church (Walter).

reduced. The orders were replaced by an ecclesiatical bureaucracy which, at least nominally, was capable of administering to an indigenous population that had acquiesced to colonial civil society, accepted a lowly status in the social system, and had, at least superficially, become assimilated into it.

The custodial transfer of religious affairs in Indian and mestizo peasant communities from the missionary orders to a secular ecclesiastical bureaucracy generally weakened the bond between the Catholic Church and its grass roots membership. Further, it left the churches established by the missionaries without a maintenance framework that directly linked communities to a tightly-knit religious hierarchy committed to church-oriented community life.

Still, local church life survived. And, through the dedication of local parish communities and secular clergy, many of the historic churches with roots in the missionary period also survived. The challenge of the future will be to preserve these beautiful old buildings from the ravages of time and careless tourism. At this point there is no effective plan to accomplish this goal. There exists, however, transnational regional organizations such as the Arizona-Mexico Commission which are in a position to apply themselves to this endeavor. Hopefully, this will be done and these churches will continue to reflect the unique heritage of the Borderlands in the pleasingly visible way that they do today.

Traveling to the Sonoran Missions
C ᵐ

Mexico is a rapidly modernizing country. The North America Free Trade Agreement (NAFTA) has added a significant measure of dynamicism to the rate of change. Obstacles and nuisances associated with road travel between the United States and Mexico and within Mexico itself are diminishing constantly. Still, traveling in Mexico presents some unique challenges that will not disappear overnight. This appendix deals with these challenges, as they exist today.

Currency

It is useful to carry enough Mexican currency to pay for essential expenses. Even though U.S. dollars are acceptable for most purchases, local merchants often give less than the official rate of exchange for purchases in dollars. Mexican pesos can be purchased before your trip, at fair rates, in Arizona. Major credit cards are honored in many modern establishments along Mexican National Highways #2 and #15 but less commonly elsewhere. National Highway #15 is a toll road. U.S. currency is accepted at tollbooths, but at less than the official exchange rate.

Accommodations

The availability of overnight accommodations in northern Sonora is more limited than in most of the United States. Comfortable and modern rooms can be found in the border towns of Agua Prieta and Nogales and in Magdalena, Santa Ana, Caborca, Hermosillo, and Cananea. Otherwise, accommodations are generally below the standards acceptable to most U.S. tourists.

Personal Identification

To travel beyond the immediate border area, i.e., more than 15 miles into the Mexican interior, you will need a tourist travel visa. These are available at some travel agencies in the United States, at Mexican Consulates, at border crossing stations (Mexican side), and at roadside control points in the Mexican interior. When obtained in the United States, tourist visas still require validation stamping at a border crossing station or at a roadside control point in Mexico.

The single best document for verifying your identification for the purpose of obtaining a tourist visa is a passport. If you lack a passport, you will have to present some combination of picture identification and proof of citizenship, e.g., birth certificate, voter's registration card. The best source for the most current information on documentation requirements is a Mexican embassy or consulate. The Mexican Consulate in Tucson is at 553 South Stone Avenue. The phone number is (520)882-5595.

Visiting Specific Sities

Historic churches are, for the most part, places of local worship and are not operated for tourism. They are generally open during the morning until noon and after 4:00 P.M.. Some, like the Pitiquito church, may be open during the early afternoons. The Oquitoa church is only opened for specific local parish activities. Visitors, when entering, should always be sensitive to religious activities taking place inside. As these churches are mostly maintained by their local parishioners, donations to their upkeep are always appreciated.

Tours

The only practical way of traveling to the Sonoran missions is by motor vehicle. There is no public transportation net that is practicable for a tourist's needs. The simplest means of visiting the Sonoran missions is through an organized tour. There are a number of organizations based in southern Arizona which operate mission tours. Tucson is the best single point of departure. In Tucson, Pima Community College (telephone: 520/625-5063), the Southwestern Mission Research Center (telephone: 520/621-4927) and Adventures in Education, Inc. (telephone: 520/795-6499) offer tours. Cochise County College in Douglas, Arizona is another source.

Personal Touring

Obviously, there are advantages to traveling independently of groups and without established itineraries. Taking your personal car is a viable option. Renting a car or van from an agency is another one. While the larger national rental agencies have been reluctant to authorize Mexico travel with their vehicles, local agencies have been more flexible. As of this book's publication date, six Tucson agencies were advertising the availability of Mexican car rentals.

Obtaining gasoline is no longer a problem in Mexico. Gasoline stations are being built everywhere and can even be found in most small communities. Dollars are accepted. Finding unleaded gas has also ceased being a significant problem except between Cananea and Banámichi and along dirt roads. In these cases, the problem is avoided if you start out with a full tank of gas.

It is important to obtain Mexican car insurance, whether driving your own car or a rental vehicle into Mexico. While this is not a formal requirement for entry, it is a practical necessity in view of even the remotest possibility of a traffic accident. If you are the driver of a non-Mexican insured car that is involved in an accident in which there is damage or injury, the vehicle will be impounded and you will be detained pending an investigation of responsibility and liability. Clearly, this is a situation to be avoided, especially since obtaining short-term Mexican insurance is easy and relatively inexpensive. Look in the local Yellow Pages in Tucson or any border town.

While the maps and other information provided herein will enable you to undertake a trip into Mexico without a guide, some things should be considered in determining whether or not to pursue this option:

• Communication can be a problem if you speak no Spanish. Some Spanish language capability is especially important in the rural countryside where many of the missions are found.

The Mexican road net connecting the missions varies considerably in quality. Roads range in character from all-weather highway such as Federal Highway #15 (above) to rural dirt tracks. Even paved roads like the main road between Cananea and Arizpe (below) can become impassable to regular passenger cars during the summer and winter rainy seasons (Walter).

• Mexico requires that all vehicles traveling in the interior (more than 15 miles beyond the border) be registered. To do this, you will need the following:

- Your driver's license.

- A copy of your vehicle registration or title, or notarized authorization from any lienholder (if this pertains). If the vehicle is not registered in your name, you will need the notarized written permission of the owner. If you are driving a rental car, you will need a copy of the rental agreement in your name, authorizing you to travel in Mexico.

- Your passport or travel visa.

- A major credit card (MC, Visa, American Express, or Diner's Club). A fee of approximately $12.00 will be billed to your credit card. Without a credit card, you will have to obtain a bond based on the blue book value of your vehicle.

Notes: Vehicle registration is accomplished at roadside control points inside Mexico. Control points are located roughly 15 miles (or 21 kilometers) into the Mexican interior. This registration is valid for repeat visits for a period of six months. However, prior to the end of the six-month period, you must cancel the registration at a control point or risk penalty under Mexican law and additional charges to your credit card.

As of the print date of this book, the Mexican Government is considering eliminating the vehicle registration fee/bond requirement. The Mexican Embassy, a consulate, or one of the mentioned group travel sources can provide updated information on this matter.

• Roadside emergency service and car repair facilities are minimal in Sonora between major population centers. If you are driving, make sure that your car has been thoroughly checked by a trustworthy mechanic beforehand. It is always useful to bring along an extra fan belt, basic tools, and common roadside emergency items (e.g., water, disabled vehicle sign). While a mobile emergency road service known as the Green Angels patrol major highways during daylight hours, you might have a long wait for them. The Green Angels do not regularly patrol most of the secondary road net that connects the missions.

• Most of the roads leading to the missions are good. However, some become impassable during rainy seasons to vehicles without 4-wheel drive and high clearance because of washouts and running water across roadways. This is especially true of the road between Cananea and Arizpe and dirt roads, as indicated on the maps herein. Rainy seasons are July through September and November through March.

• Night driving should be avoided if possible. Mexican vehicles sometimes operate without functioning stop lights or turn indicators. Broken-down vehicles are sometimes left in roadways because of the lack of shoulders and emergency parking pull-offs. Reflective or luminous warning signs are not in common use. Animals sometimes enter roadways and become collision hazards.

Having pointed out the pitfalls, let me end on a comforting note. I have found Sonorans to be friendly and helpful in assisting disabled travelers. And, perhaps because repair stations are relatively uncommon, Sonorans are resourceful in dealing with common mechanical problems.

Appendix B
Glossary
C

Cabecera	A mission headquarters and residence for a missionary responsible for the missionary activity of a district.
Corbel	A physical architectural feature that projects horizontally from within a wall to support a ceiling, beam, rafter or arch.
Cruciform	Formed or arranged in a cross.
Lintel	A physical architectural feature that horizontally spans and carries the load above such openings as windows and doorways.
Nave	The main hall or central aisle of a church.
Pimería Alta	The name given by the Spaniards to the land in the north Sonora Desert region occupied by Pima Indians.
Pilaster	An upright feature that is structurally a pier, but architecturally treated as a column and that usually projects a third of its width or less from the wall.
Retablo	The decorative architectural support or screen located behind an altar that provides a framework for the display of oil paintings, sculpture, and/or other religious objects.
Temple	A Synonym for "church".
Transept	The side wing of a church.
Viga	A ceiling beam.
Visita	A mission station maintained by local lay people and visited by a missionary on a recurring basis.

Appendix C
Chronology of Key Events

	Spain/Mexico	England/United States
1536	Vaca completes journey thru present-day U.S. Southwest	
1539	Niza explores into present-day Arizona, New Mexico	
1562	Completion of Coronado expedition reaching north to present-day Kansas	
1591	First Jesuit mission established in northwest New Spain (in Sinaloa)	
1607		Virginia colony established (Jamestown)
1620		Massachusetts colony established (Plymouth)
1630's	Jesuits reach Ures, begin work in Sonora, San Miguel Valleys	
1640's	Jesuits begin work in Moctezuma, Bavispe Valleys	
1648	Jesuits reach Arizpe	
1682		Georgia (last of 13 original colonies) established
1687	Kino arrives in Upper Pimería, enters Magdalena Valley	
1690	Kino enters Altar Valley	
1691	Kino enters present-day Arizona	
1695	First Pima revolt	
1700	Mission established near Tucson	
1751	Second Pima revolt	
1754		Beginning of 9-year "French & Indian War"
1767	Expulsion of Jesuits	
1776	San Francisco colony (California) established	Declaration of Independence
1781		British defeated at Yorktown
1803		Louisiana Purchase
1821	Mexican Independence	Treaty with Spain transfers rights to Florida & western territories
1834	Missions secularized	
1846	-------------- War between Mexico and the United States -------------- (Results in vast cession of lands to U.S.)	
1853	------------- Gadsden Purchase ------------- (Results in establishment of current U.S.-Mexican Border)	

References

Ahlborn, Richard E. Saints of San Xavier. Tucson: Southwestern Mission Research Center, Inc., 1974.

Bannon, John Francis. The Spanish Borderlands Frontier, 1513-1821. Albuquerque: University of New Mexico Press, 1974.

Donohue, John Augustine, S.J. After Kino: Jesuit Missions in Northwestern New Spain. Sources & Studies for the History of the Americas: Vol. 6. St. Louis: St. Louis University, 1969.

Eckhart, George B. "Missions of Sonora." Arizona and the West Vol.2 No.2, Summer 1960, Tucson: University of Arizona Press.

Eckhart, George B. and James S. Griffith. Temples of the Wilderness: Spanish Churches of Northern Sonora. Arizona Historical Society Monograph No.3. Tucson: Arizona Historical Society, 1975.

Fontana, Bernard. "Biography of a Desert Church: The Story of Mission San Xavier Del Bac." The Smoke Signal. No.3. Tucson: Tucson Corral of the Westerners, 1961.

_____. Entrada: The Legacy of Spain & Mexico in the United States. Tucson: Southwest Parks and Monuments Association, 1994.

Kessell, John L. Mission of Sorrows: Jesuit Guévavi and the Pimas, 1691-1767. Tucson: University of Arizona Press, 1970.

Lavender, David. De Soto, Coronado, Cabrillo: Explorers of the Northern Mystery. National Park Handbook 144.Washington, D.C. U.S. Department of the Interior, 1992.

McCarty, Kieran. Desert Documentary: The Spanish Years, 1767-1822. Tucson: Arizona Historical Society, 1976.

Meyer, Michael C. and William L. Sherman. The Course of Mexican History. 3rd ed. New York: Oxford University Press, 1987.

Nentvig, Juan, S.J. Rudo Ensayo: A Description of Sonora and Arizona in 1764. Translated, clarified, and annotated by Alberto Francisco Pradeau and Robert R. Rassmussen. Tucson: The University of Arizona Press, 1980.

Nuñez, Juan. "Bacadéhuachi," Unpublished papers, n.d.

Officer, James E. Hispanic Arizona, 1536-1856. Tucson:
The University of Arizona Press, 1989.

Pfefferkorn, Ignaz. Sonora: A Description of The Province. Translated and
annotated by Theodore E. Truetlein. Tucson: The University of Arizona
Press, 1989.

Pickens, Buford (ed.) The Missions of Northern Sonora: A 1935 Field
Documentation. Tucson: The University of Arizona Press, 1993.

Polzer, Charles W. Kino Guide II; His Missions - His Monuments. Tucson:
Southwestern Mission Research Center, 1932.

_____. "The Franciscan Entrada Into Sonora, 1645-1652: A Jesuit Chronicle,"
Arizona and the West, 14(3), 1972.

Roca, Paul M. Paths of the Padres Through Sonora. Tucson:
Arizona Historical Society, 1967.

Scheutz-Miller, Mardith and Bernard L. Fontana. "Mission Churches of
Northern Sonora," Unpublished manuscript, n.d.

Spicer, Edward H. Cycles of Conquest. Tucson: University of Arizona Press,
1962.

West, Robert C. Sonora: Its Geographical Personality. Austin:
University of Texas Press, 1993.